Donated to the Library of

Sybil Ruth Smith

Albert/Smith Book Club

Happy Reading

"Parenting Prodigals"

"Train up a child in the way he should go
and when he is old he will not depart from it."

Proverbs 22:6

Chug, chug, chug. Puff, puff, puff ~~ All ABOARD!

Donated by Vickie Gail Story Albert

June 2010

Parenting PRODIGALS

Parenting PRODIGALS

SIX PRINCIPLES FOR BRINGING YOUR
SON OR DAUGHTER BACK TO GOD

PHIL WALDREP WITH PAT SPRINGLE
FOREWORD BY DAVID JEREMIAH

Second printing

Published in the United States by Baxter Press, Friendswood, Texas. Cover design by Ruth Bochte, Phil Waldrep Ministries, Trinity, Alabama. Formatted by Anne McLaughlin, Blue Lake Design, Dickinson, Texas. Edited by Stan Campbell, Woodridge, Illinois.

ISBN: 1-888237-36-8

The version of the Bible used in this book is the New King James Version.

For the three most precious people in my life:
Debbie, Maegan, and Melodi.

TABLE OF CONTENTS

13	Foreword	
15	Chapter 1	"What Did I Do Wrong?"
33	Chapter 2	Types of Prodigals
61	Chapter 3	Principle #1: Learn to Live Guilt-Free
81	Chapter 4	Principle #2: Ask for Forgiveness
117	Chapter 5	Principle #3: Love Your Child Unconditionally
147	Chapter 6	Principle #4: Allow Sin to Run Its Course
183	Chapter 7	Principle #5: Guard Your Words
205	Chapter 8	Principle #6: Pray Specifically
225	Chapter 9	Two Joys
247	Using *Parenting Prodigals* in Classes and Groups	
251	Let Us Share Your Burden	
252	About the Author	
254	About Phil Waldrep Ministries	
256	Resources	

ACKNOWLEDGEMENTS

Authors write books for different reasons. Some writers have a story to tell or a point of view to express. Other authors find a subject so interesting that they feel they must share the fruit of their research. Still other people take pen in hand because a message burns with passion in their hearts.

This is a book born in passion. For years I heard countless individuals plead with me to pray for their son or daughter who was away from God. Their voices echoed the desperation and helplessness in their hearts. Someone had to say something. Even more importantly, someone had to offer hope.

Motivated by a desire to help, my journey for answers took me through numerous books, articles, and tapes. It was not until I interviewed several prodigals—those who have returned to serve God as well as some who still live in the "far country"—that I began to find insights to help our sons and daughters return to God. These insights carried me back to the prodigal son in Luke 15, and it was viewing that story through the eyes and actions of the father that I discovered the six principles in this book.

Along the way of preparing these materials, I realized that many people in my life deserve more expressions of gratitude than I could ever give. I want to express my sincere and heart-felt thanks . . .

To my parents, Linnes and Burnell Waldrep, who practiced these principles and prevented me from being a prodigal.

To my extended family of relatives who pray for me and are among my strongest supporters.

To the staff of Phil Waldrep Ministries who make my work a joy and not a chore.

To our graphic artist Ruth Bochte, who creatively designed the cover and Charlie Seifried of Charlie Seifried Photography for the use of his photographs. You both are blessed with creativity more than you know.

To my pastor, Dr. Mark Tolbert, and my family of faith, the Central Baptist Church in Decatur, Alabama, for their continued love, acceptance, and encouragement.

To the many churches and ministries who have partnered with us in ministry.

To the pastors, staff, and ministry leaders who continue to bring groups to our conferences.

To the prodigals who shared their stories and gave me helpful suggestions.

To my friend, Pat Springle, who used his professional skills to help me express my message clearly.

And last, but not the least, to my wife, Debbie, and our two daughters, Maegan and Melodi, who make being a husband and father the greatest honor and joy in the world.

This book leaves the presses with a prayer in our hearts for you and your prodigal. It is our sincere desire to help you experience the joy of "killing the fatted calf" when your prodigal comes home.

Phil Waldrep
Trinity, Alabama
July 1, 2001

FOREWORD

One of the greatest problems facing evangelicals in today's culture is the disconnect between generations. Truths held dear by one generation are being jettisoned by the next. Sometimes the younger generation points their finger at the lack of integrity in the lifestyle of their parents. But often, there is no perceptible cause-and-effect relationship.

Like the young man from the New Testament who demanded his inheritance and took off for the far country, many of our young people today are simply denying their spiritual heritage and choosing to live apart from the Lord.

It is easy to diagnose the problem. It is not as easy to provide a solution, but Phil Waldrep has done an excellent job in his book, *Parenting Prodigals*. His six principles provide insight, encouragement, and hope for every parent or grandparent who loves a prodigal.

My association with Phil Waldrep through Phil Waldrep Ministries has led me to expect nothing but excellence from whatever he does. *Parenting Prodigals* certainly measures up to his high standard. From the heart and perspective of a caring servant, Phil Waldrep has taken a problem that is often neglected and given it the serious treatment it deserves.

Whether you find yourself parenting a prodigal, or you know someone who is, I guarantee that this book will bring help and hope. Read it prayerfully and ask God to give you the courage to implement its life-changing principles.

Dr. David Jeremiah
Turning Point Ministries
San Diego, California
July 5, 2001

⬦

CHAPTER 1

"WHAT DID I DO WRONG?"

*W*herever I go, I meet men and women who have lost someone they love. No, the person isn't dead, but the pain of the loss is just as intense. They have lost a prodigal: a son or daughter, a grandchild, or a sister or a brother who has walked away from God and the family. After I spoke on this topic at a church a short time ago, a lady wrote me this letter.

> Dear Phil,
>
> I am writing you this letter this morning because my heart is very heavy. I've been carrying a burden for a long time, and I don't know where to turn for help. I've wanted to talk to people in my church about it, but if I do, I'm afraid it will become the subject of gossip. I'm not sure I can stand that, so I'm sharing my heart with you, hoping you can give me some advice. You spoke in our church a few months ago, and we enjoyed listening to you very much. After church, you came to our house for lunch. You saw a photograph of my husband and me with our five grown sons, and you asked

about them. For the next few minutes, I told you about them—well, about four of them, anyway. The three oldest live with their wives and children in Birmingham, where they were born and grew up before my husband was transferred. They are all fine young men, very much involved in their churches. Our youngest son married a pretty girl, a Methodist, and they now attend a Methodist church in Jackson. (I tease him that now he's a missionary to the Methodists.)

But Phil, I didn't tell you anything about our fourth son, Morris. Either you didn't notice, or you were gracious enough not to ask. Like the other boys, he grew up in church. Every time the doors were open, we were there. He heard the message of Christ loudly, clearly, and often. Morris was a loveable boy, and he sang in the choir. He volunteered to speak at every year's Youth Sunday. In fact, when the boys were young, I told my friends that he would be the one who would become a preacher or a missionary. He had such a sweet spirit.

> **I'm not sure what it was, but something turned his heart cold.**

After Morris graduated from high school, he went to college. For the first couple of years, he remained faithful to God, but then, something happened. I'm not sure what it was, but something turned his heart cold. When he came home on some weekends, we noticed that he didn't sing the hymns, and he backed away from my friends he had hugged only a few months before. I thought this was just one of those "phases" we hear about.

A few weeks later, a friend called us. His daughter went to the same university, and she had told her parents that Morris had been drinking and partying a lot. We were shocked, but when we tried to talk to him about it, he shook his head. He didn't want to talk about his drinking. Instead, he dropped a bomb on us. He told us that he was getting married—in two weeks. You guessed it. She was pregnant.

Morris quit college just before his senior year. His wife had the baby and they seemed to be doing well, considering the circumstances. After about two years, though, he told his wife he didn't love her any more, and he moved out. We found out later that he was having an affair with a woman he worked with.

He moved to get farther away from us and from his wife and child. We see him about every three months, and we talk to him on the phone almost every week, but he has made it clear that he doesn't want to talk to us about the Lord, church, or his decisions that have caused us and him so much pain. We recently learned that he is living with a woman, and they aren't married.

Phil, I'm struggling. How can a child grow up hearing the message of the gospel, have four brothers who love God and parents who would die for him, and end up so far away from God? Isn't there a verse in the Bible that says if we had raised him right he'd be serving the Lord today? I'm sure I've heard people quote that verse many times over the years, and it cuts my heart like a knife. What I really want to know is, what did I do wrong, and what can we do now to help our son return to God? Even if you don't have any advice, would you please pray for us?

> How can a child grow up hearing the message of the gospel, have four brothers who love God and parents who would die for him, and end up so far away from God?

Thank you for reading my letter and sharing our pain.

Sincerely yours,
Dorothy

This letter, with slight variations, could be written by countless parents who have the same anguished hearts. Some would change "sons" to "daughters," or have two children instead of five, or be facing a problem with drugs or jail instead of an unwanted pregnancy. But many people have a son, a daughter, a grandchild, or a sibling who has walked away from God. They have many wonderful things in their lives and are grateful for those blessings, but one person's spiritual drifting has brought tremendous heartache to the family.

You may have asked the same questions this dear lady asked in her letter: How can it happen to us? What did I do wrong? And what can I do now to bring my beloved prodigal back to God? We receive many letters at our office, but by far, the most common request is for us to pray for a wayward son or daughter, son-in-law or daughter-in-law.

THE SEARCH FOR INSIGHT

After reading the letter, I wanted to address this issue of parenting prodigals, so I researched books and sermons to find principles to share with dear parents. I found scores of books and talks on how to help rebellious children and adolescents, but I couldn't find anything on how to parent adult prodigals. That posed a problem for me. I couldn't find good, biblical research, and I felt the Lord was calling me to address this crucial need. Yet I'm a relatively young man with two daughters still in elementary and high schools. When I was a young, unmarried preacher, I often told people confidently and boldly how to raise their kids. Then Debbie and I married, and God gave us two wonderful children, Maegan and Melodi. With experience came wisdom, and I learned a thing or two—including the need to be careful about speaking authoritatively on subjects I hadn't personally encountered.

Since I couldn't share life experiences with prodigals of my own, I concluded that I needed to back away from this issue. God's Spirit, however, reminded me that He had called me to this ministry and would guide me. The Lord led me to talk to a group of men and women to hear first-hand why they had walked away from God, as well as many other one-time prodigals who had returned to the faith. Out of the rich abundance of these conversations arose some clear principles that I want to share with you.

JESUS' STORY ABOUT A PRODIGAL

Before I share these principles, though, I think it is important for us to examine the best-known prodigal in the world—the young man described in the story of the Prodigal Son. He is the figure who has caused many of us to redefine the very word *prodigal*. To be technical about the definition, "prodigal" means "rashly or wastefully extravagant." As we will see, this was certainly true of the young man in the parable. Because of the power of this story, we have come to speak of a *prodigal* as a runaway, of someone who remains distant from home and from those who love him. This will be how the word is used throughout this book.

Jesus, while surrounded by many tax collectors and sinners, had been speaking about the Father's love and acceptance. Also in attendance were the Pharisees and scribes who followed the letter of the law and were disgusted that Jesus would hang out with such riff-raff. They condemned Him along with the other outcasts of society.

In response to the Pharisees' implicit criticism of God's gracious forgiveness, Jesus told three parables, each about the joy of finding something that had been lost. He told about a shepherd finding a lost sheep, a woman finding a lost coin, and a father reuniting with his "lost" son. Each of these three parables communicated the same powerful message: just as human parents ache at the loss of a prodigal child, our heavenly Father longs for His lost children to return to Him.

We usually call this third story the "Parable of the Prodigal Son," but it could just as easily be titled the "Parable of the Wonderful Father." Luke records Jesus' words: "A certain man had two sons. And the younger of them said to his father, 'Father, give me the portion of goods that falls to me.' And he divided to them his livelihood" (Luke 15:11-12). In that day, two-thirds of a man's estate was given to the principal heir, and the remaining third was divided among the other sons. Since there were only two sons, the second son would receive one-third of the estate. However, heirs normally didn't receive their inheritance until the father died or could no longer manage it.[1] The request of the younger son in Jesus' story was unusual, if not inappropriate. Still, the father gave him a portion of the estate as he had requested.

The young man converted his newly acquired possessions into cash so he could travel. Luke continues, "And not many days after, the younger son gathered all together, journeyed to a far country, and there wasted his possessions with prodigal living" (Luke 15:13). With a wallet full of money, he headed for the Middle Eastern equivalent of New Orleans, straight for Bourbon Street! If you wonder what this young man spent his money doing, you need look no farther than the nightclubs and red-light districts of your own town, but this son didn't want to stay close to home. He traveled to "a far country" where he could indulge himself away from his father's watchful eyes.

1 John F. Walvoord and Roy B. Zuck, *The Bible Knowledge Commentary*, (Victor Books, Wheaton, Illinois, 1983) p. 245.

Luke tells us that things didn't go well for the young man: "But when he had spent all, there arose a mighty famine in that land, and he began to be in want. And he went and joined himself to a citizen of that country, and he sent him into his fields to feed swine. And he would gladly have filled his stomach with the pods that the swine ate, and no one gave him anything" (Luke 15:14-16).

> **Suddenly, his fun had turned to famine and his pals turned to pigs!**

Notice that he ran out of money just as a famine hit the land. A coincidence? No, I don't think so. God orchestrates all kinds of events, even calamities, to get our attention. The son was now desperate, but not desperate enough to go home. Instead, he sent out some job applications, finding only the opportunity to feed pigs. He was away from the Land of Promise and had turned his back on the sacred covenant with God that his family and his people upheld. He had been a well-to-do young man enjoying life in his father's home, but now he was feeding hogs in a foreign land! Nothing could be worse for a Jewish man. He was so hungry that he longed for the food the pigs ate, but he was friendless—desperate and alone. Suddenly, his fun had turned to famine and his pals turned to pigs!

In the meantime, what do you suppose the father was thinking? The son wasn't away for just a weekend excursion. It would have taken many months or even years to squander a third of the wealth of an estate. As the days and months passed, the father may have wondered, "What did I do wrong? Why did my son want to leave?

Was I foolish to let him take his inheritance too soon?" But there were no answers yet.

The young man was doing his best to make it, but his life simply was a disaster. He was devastated . . . broken. That very brokenness, however, was a prerequisite for insight. Jesus explained, "And when he came to himself, he said, 'How many of my father's hired servants have bread enough and to spare, and I perish with hunger! I will arise and go to my father, and will say to him: Father, I have sinned against heaven and before you, and I am no longer worthy to be called your son. Make me like one of your hired servants' " (Luke 15:17-19). Only in his abject brokenness did the once proud young man think of home. Only when he became utterly destitute did he realize how much he needed to repent and return to his father.

Some of us think, "If I can just get my prodigal to read this book, or listen to that tape, or go to church, then he'll change." We nag and plead, but our efforts only drive our prodigals farther away. The son in Jesus' story had to come to the end of his rope. He had to become utterly and completely helpless and hopeless before he "came to himself." Self-discovery is a very lonely and difficult course, but for most prodigals, it is the only path back. No one else can help them until they are ready to face some harsh realities.

The depth of the son's repentance is seen in the speech he prepared for his father. He wasn't asking to be restored as a son, only as a hired servant who would enjoy the privileges of food and shelter. That would be welcome relief, and enough grace to satisfy him.

I can envision the father on his knees day after day, pleading with God to bring his son home. His pillow probably was stained with his tears from crying every night. And every day he peered down the dirt road that led up to the house. Some day, maybe today, he would see his son walking up that road. Every day he reflected on his decision to let his son leave. Maybe he had made a mistake by giving his son an early inheritance, maybe not. That's not the point of Jesus' story. The real point is found in the next scene after the young man turned toward home. "And he arose and came to his father. But when he was still a great way off, his father saw him and had compassion, and ran and fell on his neck and kissed him" (Luke 15:20).

Can you imagine what the son thought as he saw his father running toward him? He may have imagined that his father was furious with him for acting so stupidly and wasting all he had worked so hard for. I can imagine terror in the young man's eyes! But the father's heart contained no rage or criticism. Instead, he embraced his son and kissed him.

Startled at first, the son began his prepared speech. "And the son said to him, 'Father, I have sinned against heaven and in your sight, and am no longer worthy to be called your son.' But the father said to his servants, 'Bring out the best robe and put it on him, and put a ring on his hand and sandals on his feet. And bring the fattened calf here and kill it, and let us eat and be merry; for this my son was dead and is alive again; he was lost and is found.' And they began to be merry" (Luke 15:21-24).

Do you know what I love about this passage? The father didn't even let his son finish his speech. All he needed to know was that his son was back and was repentant. The father was so excited to welcome him back that he interrupted him to send his servants to run errands of joy.

The father's instructions to his servants are very important. The best robe in the house was reserved for an honored guest. The ring signified that his position of sonship, which he forfeited when he left, was being reinstated. Sandals were worn by family members; slaves went barefoot. The fattened calf was always ready for special occasions

> **The father's outburst of orders may have been spontaneous, but then again, they may have been rehearsed a thousand times before as he looked down that road hoping to see a glimpse of his son returning home.**

when special guests dropped in unexpectedly or when there was an unusual cause for celebration. The father's outburst of orders may have been spontaneous, but then again, they may have been rehearsed a thousand times before as he looked down that road hoping to see a glimpse of his son returning home. Perhaps this flood of joy and celebration had been secretly planned in the father's heart for a long, long time.

When his son returned, the father had every reason to take out his ledger book and say, "OK, you're back. Good to see you. Now, let's see what you need to do to pay back all you squandered." Or he could have yelled at the boy for being so foolish. But there was neither a harsh word nor a look of condemnation. Not one. The father's pride may have been hurt by his son's actions. People at the Temple may have gossiped that their kids certainly would never do what his son had done, and their snickers may have cut him deeply. But whatever mixed feelings the father experienced during those years had been prayed through so that only love and compassion remained.

There was, however, a different problem. The elder son heard the celebration and came in from the fields where he had been serving his father faithfully day after day. When he saw that his father was showering his wayward brother with gifts and grace, jealousy flamed in his heart. He barked at his father, "It's unfair! How can you welcome him back and give him such gifts? I've served you all this time, and you've never done that for me!"

It is a wonderful and glorious thing when a prodigal comes back home, but the return may open wounds we had no idea even existed. Rivalry may be normal, but it can be deadly. When parents compare one child to another, they set up a "good kid" and "bad kid" competition. Even though the "good kid" wins all the time in the comparison game, that competition robs the family of grace and love. The parents, and the children, too, lose their objectivity and develop "black and white" thinking: one is all bad and the other is all good.

The pain parents feel because of a prodigal often causes them to believe the "bad kid" can do no right and the "good kid" can do no wrong. If the prodigal repents and returns, this comparison makes it even harder to forgive him. And if they find the grace to forgive, the "good kid" may be resentful of the grace shown to the "bad kid." Instead of joy, bitterness reigns in the household. In Jesus' story, the elder brother was the "good kid," and he knew it. In fact, he was proud of the fact that he hadn't been as foolish as his brother. He had compared himself to his brother, and he felt self-righteous and superior. When his father showed compassion, jealousy and bitterness filled his heart.

Jesus told this story to the Pharisees and scribes who were complaining that He spent time showing love to the "bad kids" of that city—the tax collectors and prostitutes. The message of the parable is not just about the wonderful grace of the Father, but also about the bitterness of those who were rigid, demanding, and self-righteous. In a prodigal's family, every family member needs the grace of God:

- The prodigal needs to come to his senses and repent;
- The parents need to forgive the prodigal for the deep pain he has inflicted; and
- Other family members need to open their hearts to forgive and love the prodigal so bitterness, self-righteousness, and jealousy don't ruin their lives.

GRANDPARENTS AND SIBLINGS, TOO

As I have talked with people across the country about parenting prodigals, I have learned that these principles relate not only to parents, but to grandparents and siblings, too. Many grandparents anguish over the behavior of their grandkids. The parents don't seem to be able to reach them, and the grandparents feel they have a special opportunity to touch their prodigal grandchildren's broken lives. And many brothers and sisters of prodigals apply these principles, as well.

A friend has a brother who is an alcoholic and gambling addict. He told me his mother just closes her eyes to his brother's behavior and acts like "everything's fine." My friend, however, has watched his brother ruin his life and inflict pain on everyone around him. He desperately wants to help his brother turn his life around.

> The principles we will examine in these pages challenge us to be honest with ourselves and realize there are limits to what we can do to change other people. Some of us are reading this book as a last resort.

The principles we will examine in these pages challenge us to be honest with ourselves and realize there are limits to what we can do to change other people. Some of us are reading this book as a last resort. We are afraid it's too late; our beloved prodigals, we believe, have gone too far down the wrong road to ever turn back. Let me assure you, it's never too late. God is a God of miracles, and sometimes His miracles begin within us before He changes those we love.

In the next chapter, we will look at several different types of prodigals to help us understand who they are and how they think about God, about themselves, and about us. Along the way, I will illustrate the different types of prodigals and demonstrate the principles in action. Once we understand the mind of the prodigal, we will be ready to apply the principles of bringing him or her back to God.

Note: At the end of each chapter you will find questions and exercises to help you apply the principles in that chapter. You may want to write your responses in the space provided, or you may choose to write in your own devotional journal. Take your time. Think, pray, and let God's Spirit give you insight and encouragement.

A CLOSER LOOK . . .

1.   In what ways do you identify with the lady who wrote the letter to me at the beginning of this chapter?

2.   As you think about the father in the parable of the Prodigal Son, what encourages you about his character and actions?

What are some things he did right?

What, if anything, did he do wrong?

How would you have handled the son's request for his share of the inheritance?

What aspects of the father's attitude and actions challenge you?

3. What do you hope God will do in your life as a result of reading this book?

4. I invite you to write a prayer asking God to have His way in you and in your prodigal.
    Dear Lord . . .

❖

TYPES OF PRODIGALS

$\mathcal{W}$ hen we think of prodigals, we usually think of the angry, defiant children who run away from home and turn their backs on the things we value. Certainly, that type is perhaps most visible, but there are other varieties that break our hearts just as much. In this chapter, we will examine several types of prodigals: those who are embarrassing, defiant, intellectual, lukewarm, and religious.

EMBARRASSING PRODIGALS

An embarrassing prodigal may be a son in jail, a daughter who is living with a man she's not married to, an unwed mother, or a homosexual who has "come out of the closet" to his parents' consternation. The embarrassing prodigal is a prime candidate for gossip. As parents, we are often defensive and evasive when people ask about this type of child because we realize (or suspect) that behind our backs, our "friends" talk about the foolishness of the child

> **The embarrassing prodigal is a prime candidate for gossip.**

and what sins we must have committed to create the situation.

I know a man whose son is serving ten years for burglary in the state prison and often works on the highway "chain gang." When those who aren't familiar with this father's pain ask about his children, he tells about the vocations of each of his other three children. If asked about his other son, he says that he "works for the state."

A woman had a cousin who was gay—a secret the family kept for years. But when the young man finally began to tell other people, his family members didn't know how to react. When together, they talked about everything and everybody else, and some avoided even the mention of his name. They felt both shame and incomprehension of how something like that could happen. In a few years, the man died of AIDS, and not even his death united the family. Some felt compassion for his wasted life and attended the graveside service. A few attended out of guilt because they hadn't reached out to him. Others stayed away because they didn't want to be seen at a funeral where there would be other gays and lesbians who were friends of this man. In fact, the family was so embarrassed that they rushed to have him buried as soon as possible to avoid a crowd at the funeral. He died at 4 o'clock in the morning, and they buried him at 2 o'clock that afternoon.

I know of a music director who served at the church where he was raised and where his parents had attended since they were children. But after he embezzled some money, church leaders showered blame not only on him, but on his parents as well. "If he had been raised right," several of them told each other, "he wouldn't have done such an awful thing." His parents had to walk through the doors of that church, their spiritual home for their entire lives, and face accusations and gossip from those they had called their friends. These parents listened as people talked about their son as if he were a criminal seen on the evening news—and as if they weren't in the room. The words of others, though they may have been true, stung deeply.

Someone said to his father, "I know he's a grown man, but he's your son. If you're the man you ought to be, you'll write the church a check to cover what he stole." So the father did just that. While he had no moral or religious obligations to repay the debt, he didn't want the church to be hurt. He took a second mortgage on his home in order to pay the full amount because he wanted desperately to stop the accusations that were focused on his son, his wife, and himself. Paying for his son's sin was this father's way of trying to deal with his embarrassment.

But not all parents can literally pay for the wrongs their prodigals have committed. I talked with a woman whose son had been convicted of murder and executed for his crime. Through the long years of trials, appeals, trips to the prison to visit her son, and finally, that awful day when he was put to death, it seemed that everyone's compassion was focused on the victim's family, which was understandable. But this grieving mother was also losing someone she treasured. She told me through her tears, "In all those years, I don't remember anyone who came to me and told me, 'I'm praying for you. I know you're hurting.' " Instead, when people looked at her she could tell they were thinking, "Your son is getting exactly what he deserves."

There's no question that his crime had to be punished, but it hurt the mother terribly. She had to cope not only with the fact that he had committed such a crime, but also that he would lose his life as justice was meted out. Her prodigal would never come home.

Most addictions and crimes produce prodigals that embarrass the people who love them. I have talked to griev-

> **Most addictions and crimes produce prodigals that embarrass the people who love them.**

ing parents who won't talk to their friends, but they feel safe telling me about an adult child who is addicted to drugs, sex, or gambling. We are not quite as ashamed of workaholics in the family, because they at least have something to show for their patholo-gy. But sooner or later we realize that their pay raises and promotions are frequently offset by ruined family relationships. We also tend to overlook food addictions because so many other people have them, too. But some parents constantly nag an overweight child, especially a daughter, to get her to lose weight. It's one thing to always have the other person's best interests in mind, yet too often we try to control them because we are embarrassed.

DEFIANT PRODIGALS

Defiant prodigals are determined to hurt their parents. They often belittle their parents' faith. Sometimes defiance is a second step for an embarrassing prodigal as a response to the shame displayed by family members.

> **Defiant prodigals are determined to hurt their parents.**

A young woman who looked forward to a bright future after college got involved romantically with a controlling, domineering man. This young lady was a sweet Christian, the darling of her parents' eyes, but when she came under the spell of this man her personality changed radically. Initially, her parents were happy she had found someone she loved. As graduation day drew near, however, they noticed that her demeanor became more secretive and sullen. The joy went out of her face and voice. Her parents tried to tell each other that she was just nervous about graduating and going into the "real world," but they also noticed that she avoided talking to them about anything important, especially her boyfriend. Graduation day came, but she spent more and more time with her boyfriend. She didn't want to celebrate with her parents who had consistently supported her emotionally, spiritually, and financially.

She had several job offers around the state, but she turned them all down to stay in the college town with her boyfriend. When she took a job as a waitress, her parents became very concerned. They hadn't spent thousands of dollars on her education for her to now throw it away. They tried to reason with her, but she only became angry and defensive. They prayed for her and with her, but she just sat with her arms folded. They pleaded with her, but she fled to the arms of her boyfriend.

Soon she was living with him. After several tense months in the relationship, she called to tell her parents she was pregnant. Her boyfriend demanded that she get an abortion. She knew it was wrong, but still couldn't muster the courage to break away from him. She was under tremendous pressure from him to do what he wanted her to do, from her parents to get away from him, and from her own conscience which was telling her what was right. In utter despair and confusion, she exploded in rage against her parents. "You can't tell me what to do!" she yelled. "I'm on my own now, and I'll do whatever I want!" The sweet, gentle girl became an enraged, defiant unwed mother.

In a similar story, a young woman now in her 30's got sexually involved with a man when they were dating. She got pregnant, and within weeks they were married. A few years later they had two children, but the foundation of the marriage was never strong. She eventually divorced her husband and lived alone with her daughters for many years. Loneliness was too painful to endure, however, so she married a convicted felon, a man she knew her family would despise. Before the wedding, several friends and family members tried to talk her out of it, but she insisted on marrying him. The anger and resentment was so intense that many friends and members of her family refused to talk to her, but for some reason, she was willing to talk with me. I foresaw a train wreck of pressures from the marriage, but I called to congratulate her.

She was shocked and asked me, "Don't you think what I'm doing is wrong, marrying this man?"

I thought for a moment and then replied, "No, intellectually and biblically I can't tell you it's wrong. I think you, your husband, and your girls will experience tremendous heartaches because so many people disapprove of what you are doing. But I love you dearly, and there's nothing you can do that will cause me to love you any less."

She fully expected me, a preacher, to condemn her at least as much as others had, and she was shocked when I offered grace instead. Showing her kindness, I realize, is a risk. Others who prefer judgment to grace may well turn their guns on me and accuse me of "siding with her." If they choose to condemn me for reaching out to her and her husband, so be it. I want to honor the Lord by showing His kindness instead of buckling under to others' desire for vengeance. I'm willing to take that risk for the opportunity to bring reconciliation.

As we talked, I realized that her decision to marry this man may have been motivated by a desire to hurt people who had hurt her. The divorce from her first husband was very embarrassing. While she was going through that painful period, nobody reached out to her. In fact, many condemned her viciously and withdrew from her. I'm convinced that the pain of alienation and condemnation she experienced during her divorce drove her to try to punish and embarrass her friends

> **I realized that her decision to marry this man may have been motivated by a desire to hurt people who had hurt her.**

39

and family. Her method of retaliation was to marry a man others despised.

INTELLECTUAL PRODIGALS

Intellectual prodigals do not engage in overt sin. They may be wonderful, honorable people with no moral flaws. They abide by the law and are often successful in business or professional careers. They are good sons or daughters, fathers or mothers, husbands or wives. They are not embarrassing to the family, and certainly aren't defiant. In fact, their success makes their families very proud of them. Yet intellectual prodigals have abandoned their faith. Even if they showed great interest in the things of God in the past, their faith has now grown cold.

> They are not embarrassing to the family, and certainly aren't defiant. In fact, their success makes their families very proud of them.

I know a man who is a brilliant medical doctor. His parents were farmers here in the South who were determined to provide good educations for their children as the best hope for them to make a better life. In their rural environment, most everybody went to church and revered God, so this young man heard the truth from God's Word every week in church and every day around his home.

Then he left for college. On campus his faith was challenged by the humanistic concepts taught there. He listened as biology professors scoffed at the Creation story and taught the principles of evolution. Gradually, doubts took root in his heart, and his faith slowly eroded. By the time he graduated from medical school, this fine young man had no faith at all. He wasn't defiant, and he certainly wasn't an embarrassment to the family. They were very proud of his achievements and his commitment to help others.

He advanced in his profession and became the medical director of a fine hospital. Today, this renowned doctor never goes to church, though he is one of the kindest men I know. When we talk, he asks me the hard intellectual questions, such as, "How can a loving God send somebody to hell?" In addition to theological stumbling blocks, he experienced a personal and emotional blow to his faith. His mother, a good and godly woman, was diagnosed with cancer. For months, he watched helplessly as she wasted away, suffering a very painful death. Many people prayed for her to be healed, or at least to experience comfort from her intense pain, but her suffering only increased as the weeks went on. This fine doctor knew his profession couldn't help his mother, but perhaps, he desperately hoped, the prayers of the faithful could bring her peace. When she finally died after a long and painful struggle, any glimmer of faith in his heart utterly collapsed. He assumed God either wasn't there or didn't care.

Intellectual prodigals often begin questioning theology on a rational basis, but their intellect- and logic-based faith is often crushed by a deep disappointment in life. They need to see evidence, but it is often the evidence of love rather than truth that is most convincing to them.

41

They simply can't explain away people who genuinely love them.

One of the most brilliant men in NASA is a member of a church in Huntsville, Alabama. Once a confirmed and hardened atheist, today he is one of the most committed Christians in the church. Years ago, this brilliant scientist bought a farm outside of Huntsville. At work, the scientist labored over complex theories and organized extensive and complicated projects. After all this intellectual stimulation each day, he went home to do farm work. His tractor tended to break down regularly, and each time it did, his neighbor always came over and helped fix it. His neighbor was an old farmer who could not read or write, and the scientist always offered to pay the man for his trouble. But the farmer would simply reply, "No, that's OK. I did it unto the Lord." This illiterate old man was wise and discerning about the condition of this brilliant scientist's heart. He saw through the intellectual shell and looked deep into the man's troubled, empty heart. After months of building the relationship and many tractor repairs, the farmer tearfully told the scientist, "You're a lot smarter than I am, but I sure wish you knew my Lord."

For several months, the two very different men shared many hours together talking about the weather, the price of hay, and the best fertilizer to use on the fields. They also kept working on that tractor together as they learned about each other's lives. Then the scientist discovered his grown daughter was gravely ill. For perhaps the first time in his life, he began to think about life after death.

In his conversations with the farmer, he had learned that the old man's brother had been very ill, and had subsequently died. At this crucial moment in the scientist's life, he asked the old farmer about his brother's death. The farmer recalled the long, painful death his brother endured, but he didn't seem bitter at all. This touched the scientist deeply. He asked, "How can you believe in a God who lets something like that happen to your brother?"

> **He asked, "How can you believe in a God who lets something like that happen to your brother?"**

The old farmer looked at him gently and replied, "Yes, my brother died. And yes, in some ways it was tragic. But you don't understand. The Lord walked him through that pain, and I know I'm going to see my brother again someday. That's what gives me hope." The simple faith of an illiterate farmer touched the heart of this brilliant scientist, and he trusted Christ as his Savior. The farmer didn't preach to him, and he didn't rebuke him for his unbelief, but neither was he awed into silence by the scientist's fame and intelligence. He looked deep into this man's heart and saw a lost and lonely man who needed both a loving friend and a loving Savior. Thanks to the faithful farmer, the scientist received both.

If the neighbor or anyone else had tried to debate this scientist into a commitment to the faith, I doubt they would have succeeded. But love conquers all. God used this old farmer's kindness and honesty to touch the scientist's heart.

LUKEWARM PRODIGALS

Lukewarm prodigals may say the right words and appear to be right with the Lord, but they don't see the importance of being actively involved in church.

I know two brothers, Paul and James. Paul is active in church, but James is not very interested. He comes to worship sometimes, but plainly his heart isn't in it. Their father tries to shame James to being more involved in church and places pressure on him by telling him, "I told others you would be there, so don't let me down, son." On one occasion, the father tried to put the squeeze on his son by telling others he would be responsible for a task at the church. He said, "James, in Sunday School class today, I volunteered you to do the outreach. Here's the list of people to call. We're all counting on you, son."

At one point, James was trying to get a new job, and his father told him, "Son, if people know you haven't been going to church regularly, they may not give you the job you want. Think about that. We'll see you this Sunday." The father thought such manipulation would motivate his son, but it only drove his heart farther away.

Parents of lukewarm prodigals frequently withhold the blessing of

> **Parents of lukewarm prodigals frequently withhold the blessing of unconditional love and affirmation. They want their children to be on fire for the Lord (or at least to *appear* to be on fire for the Lord!), so they plead and condemn and manipulate.**

unconditional love and affirmation. They want their children to be on fire for the Lord (or at least to appear to be on fire for the Lord!), so they plead and condemn and manipulate. They don't treat them like adults and respect their choices. Of course, they claim, "I'm only doing this for his own good," but their manipulative actions and condemning attitudes are destructive, not helpful.

I talked to this James about his faith and his relationship with his parents. He told me, "When I was young, I went to Sunday School and church, and I went to services Sunday night and Wednesday night. My mother had a committee meeting Monday night, and my father went to visitation Tuesday night. I felt robbed because the church stole my parents' attention away from me." His words were a revelation to me, and I doubt his parents had any idea he felt that way. He spoke with conviction about his own values which were shaped by his painful experience. He said, "I'm not going to deny my kids the opportunity to be with me. I have to work six days a week, and I work late many nights. I don't get to see my wife and kids that often. Sunday morning is one of the best—and only—times for me to spend with them. That's why I don't go to church that often."

Many of today's prodigals are lukewarm. They work hard to succeed, and they value time with their families above everything else. They feel like they can have a relationship with God whenever it's convenient for them. Sunday mornings can be devoted to the family instead of going to church (where the services may seem pretty irrelevant to them, anyway). The older generation closely connects a relationship with God to church attendance, but the younger generation often makes a very clear distinction. They don't mind missing church because they feel they can have a rewarding relationship with God on their own terms, on their own schedule. Both groups think they're right. Unfortunately, the lukewarm prodigal fails to realize his inconsistent church attendance may actually be a reflection of an undisciplined life, rather than a genuine desire to be with his family.

RELIGIOUS PRODIGALS

People sometimes approach me with deep concerns about adult children who have gotten involved with the Jehovah's Witnesses, the Mormons, various New Age organizations, or similar religious groups. We don't usually think of such children as prodigals, yet it creates a heartbreaking situation for many parents and grand-parents to watch their grown kids get involved in a cult or false religion.

A friend of mine raised his kids in the church. He was (and is) a very devout man of God. He welcomed his children's questions about the Christian faith, and they often talked about other religions so he could teach them the differences in their beliefs. His son went to college and began dating a girl who was a Mormon. Whether out of spiritual curiosity or romantic attraction to his girlfriend, he visited the Mormon church with her. He didn't want to tell his parents he was going to a Mormon church because he was sure they would disapprove. He fully intended to stay strong in his Christian beliefs, so he boldly asked the

Mormon elders all the questions he and his father had discussed so many times. They weren't offended by his questions. In fact, they seemed to welcome them. These Mormons, he concluded, didn't seem so bad after all.

Adding to his confusion was the fact that the church where he had been attending was often embroiled in arguments and controversy, from the quality of the pastor's sermon to the color of the carpet in the Fellowship Hall. Recent disputes had escalated into shouting matches at business meetings (ending when someone actually hurled a hymnal at the meeting chairman) and having to call in sheriff's deputies to keep order. Relationships had been strained to say the least, and many members continued to hold grudges. Such experiences had quite an impact on this young man. The Mormons didn't seem to condone that kind of bickering. As far as he could tell, they loved each other, and they loved him.

We don't usually think of such children as prodigals, yet it creates a heartbreaking situation for many parents and grandparents to watch their grown kids get involved in a cult or false religion.

Soon he made some friends in that church, and he found himself going regularly with his girlfriend. He fell in love with his Mormon sweetheart, and his emotions completely blinded his search for truth. They got married and now faithfully attend the Mormon church. He might

47

not have been so quick to convert had it not been for the bickering and bitterness of his prior church.

Cults are often more open than many Christian churches to accepting those who visit. Too many of our churches are rigid and judgmental. Some of us don't want alcoholics sitting next to us. Or we don't want people who smoke cigarettes stinking up the parlor. We may look down our noses at a black man walking in with a white woman, and if their kids are out of control, that's even worse! If a woman who has been through five marriages walks through our doors, do we welcome her with open arms or scowl in self-righteousness? And what about a visitor who has been arrested for child abuse who sneaks in and sits on the back pew?

> **Who is standing at the door of your church, the loving Father or the scowling Pharisee?**

Many churches hang a sign, not on the door but on the faces of the congregation, which says, "No prodigals allowed." Religious prodigals stay in the cults because they don't believe they can return home without getting a lecture. Who is standing at the door of your church, the loving Father or the scowling Pharisee?

OUR RESPONSE TO PRODIGALS

Our embarrassing prodigals fill us with shame, and we either ignore them and hope they will change on their own, or we pester them with demands to shape up their lives. Defiant prodigals tend to prompt a corresponding defiance in us. We are infuriated by their selfishness and foolishness, and we match them yell for yell, and condemnation for condemnation. We may be proud of the success and prestige of our intellectual prodigals, but we hope someone will argue them back into the Kingdom. Lukewarm prodigals, we are sure, should know better. If we just say the right thing to get them to be more interested, they'll change. If saying the right thing doesn't work (and it doesn't), we nag them incessantly. We try to tell religious prodigals how wrong they are and shame them into coming back to the church.

So while the behavior of our prodigals usually isn't appropriate, our own actions might not be much better. Let's look at our responses a bit more closely.

Condemnation

Our intentions may be good and pure, but our words and actions too often drive our beloved prodigals even farther away from God and from us. We become angry at them for acting so foolishly—and for making us look like failures as parents. Our anger finds expression in criticism and condemnation, both toward them and anyone else who will listen, and we feel completely justified in our condemning words. After all, we tell ourselves, the person's behavior is a terrible model for others in the family, so we are taking a stand for God and for righteousness against the sinfulness of that wayward prodigal. We want to be a safeguard against others following that example, and on top of that, condemning someone who is sinning just feels right.

Self-blame

Our anger directed toward a prodigal is frequently matched with tremendous self-condemnation and guilt. We blame them for inappropriate behavior, but we also blame ourselves for not being better parents. I've talked to parents who, after telling me the horror story of their children's lives, are confused about the course they should take. They lament, "I want to trust him, but I just can't. Do you think I should anyway? Something must be terribly wrong with me that I can't trust my own child." After years of irresponsibility, embarrassing and defiant prodigals prove they are untrustworthy, yet we feel guilty for not trusting them "just one more time."

Ignoring the Problem

For some parents, the pain of facing reality is overwhelming, so we don't face it at all. We refuse to think about our prodigals, we won't talk about them, and we change the subject if somebody brings them up in conversation. I've listened as parents argued about a child who is an alcoholic. The father told me, "Our Chad has a huge problem with drinking. He's an alcoholic." But the mother wasn't able to admit as much, and shot back in anger at her husband, "How can you say that? Just because he drinks a beer or two doesn't make him an alcoholic!" The husband then recounted the times Chad has been fired from his jobs, the three failed marriages, and numerous episodes when they couldn't find him for days because he was drunk in some cheap motel—all irrefutable evidence of a binge drinker. Still, the mother clung to her illusion. "He was just looking for another job. That's all."

Some of us see the extent of our prodigals' waywardness, but we excuse them. We say, "Oh, he can't help it. He had such a difficult childhood." We list off a litany of hard times the child has endured without realizing they are similar to what most of us have experienced without becoming prodigals. It is easier for us to excuse them, though, than to hold them responsible for their actions.

Lies and Cover-ups

Most of the time we don't tell bald-faced lies about our prodigals, but we shade the truth to make the situation look better than it actually is (like the father of the chain-gang prisoner who told friends his son was "working for the state"). We blame failed marriages on the son-in-law or daughter-in-law instead of admitting that both were at fault for the breakup. We paint rosy pictures of kids looking for better jobs, but neglect to say it's because the former boss has fired them for using the company computer to look at online porn sites—again. If we tell the hard truth, we are afraid we will look like bad parents, and we don't want our friends to think of us as failures. We shade the truth to protect our prodigals' reputations in order to protect our own.

Nagging

A child is messing up his life, and by George, we know exactly how to fix it. So we tell him. Again and again, we tell him how he can be a better parent, spouse, employee, and Christian. But by the 483,392nd plea, our prodigal has learned to smile and nod while he's tuning us out. Some of us use spiritual threats to nag our children. We shake our heads and tell them they are going to suffer the fires of hell if they don't change their ways, or we warn them over and over again that they will reap what they sow.

We think we're encouraging them. We believe we are calling them to righteousness, and that we're taking a stand for godliness. We are convinced that our words and actions are in our children's best interests, and if they only change their behavior, they'll become better examples for the grandkids and have fewer problems.

Attempts to Fix the Problem

Many parents go beyond nagging to active involvement. We simply can't stand by and watch a child ruin his life, so we step in to fix the problem. This may have been appropriate when our sons and daughters were in grade school, but they are adults now, and they need to take responsibility for their own behavior. I know parents who gave a son addicted to gambling tens of thousands of dollars, and he lost every penny. When bookies came to collect, his parents wrote a check to get rid of them. When the son wanted to make a lot of money quickly in online stock trading, they gave him a "loan" to help him get started. After the brokerage firm demanded that he pay his huge debts when his margined stocks went south, the parents again paid. Scores of times, they warned him, "This is the last time we're going to give you any money," but the next time he needed it, they signed the check.

Fixers believe they are doing the right thing, or at least what is necessary to help their children. They are driven by a nagging sense of guilt: "If I'd been a better parent, my child wouldn't be in such bad shape," or "If I don't help her, who will?" And they live in fear that failing to fix a prodigal's problem may result in tragic harm. Guilt and fear are powerful motivators to keep fixers doing whatever they can do to make life better for their prodigals. Fixing an irresponsible person's predicament, however, prevents him from facing hard, cold reality. In the long run, it may keep him from repentance.

> **Fixing an irresponsible person's predicament, however, prevents him from facing hard, cold reality. In the long run, it may keep him from repentance.**

Quiet Anguish

Some of us have tried everything we know to try. We've gotten advice, and we've given advice. We've shared passages of Scripture, and we've prayed diligently. For years we've lived every day hoping our son or daughter will come down that road toward home, but the road is still empty—and our hope has turned to despair. We still long for a miracle, but we now suspect no miracle will actually come.

Perhaps our own relationships with God have been soured by disappointment. We still sing the songs and listen to the sermons, but now we secretly doubt that God is really good and sovereign like we've always believed. We don't even want to talk about the possibility of our prodigals coming home because we don't want to be disappointed again. Crushed hopes reduce our world to despairing, anguished thoughts. We feel alone—abandoned by God, our friends, and our prodigal children.

I had separate conversations with a mother and her 32-year-old son. He talked very openly about his life as a homosexual. He had regularly attended church as a child, but he told me, "I always knew I was different. I tried to date a number of times, but nothing happened. There was no spark, no romance like other people said they felt when they dated. I kind of suspected early in my life that I was going in a different direction than other people. After high school, I quit trying to be like everybody else. I knew I was gay."

"How did your mother take the news?" I asked him.

"Oh, wow! She was a basket case. At first, she was furious. She said I was 'as stupid as a box of rocks' for acting out my sexual preferences, you know, with AIDS and everything. For several years—yes, years!—she tried to tell me I was normal and I would 'come around,' but of course, I didn't. Then she went through her pleading stage when she kept asking me to go to see her pastor so he could straighten me out. I saw him a couple of times, just to appease her, but it was like trying to convince a turtle that it can fly. Words aren't enough. A turtle is just a turtle, and there's nothing wrong with that, you know."

He looked for me to approve of his logic, but I just looked at him intently. He continued, "Of course, she gave me books and articles from Exodus International, the Christian group that tries to get gay people to go straight. I appreciated her interest, but I wish she'd just accept me the way I am, like God does."

"And what's your relationship with your mother like now?" I asked him.

"We talk every week on the phone, but never, never, about my lifestyle. I guess she gave up on me. And you know, she has never mentioned it to any of her friends. As far as they know, I'm as straight as an arrow and dating some hot chicks!" He laughed at his own humor, then he became somber. "I think she's really ashamed of me. The last time we talked, she told me she must have done something really bad when I was a kid that made me turn out like this. But the truth is, she had absolutely nothing to do with it. It's just who I am, that's all."

When I asked his mother about all this, she looked at the floor and stammered, "I don't know what went wrong. We . . . we don't talk much about that anymore. I did the best I could. Maybe some day. . . ." Her guilt and shame were palpable. Lines of worry and heartache were etched on her sad face, but she had chosen to bear her burden alone.

This dear Christian lady had tried every response. She had blamed her son and herself; she had lied (and was still lying) to her friends; she had nagged her son and tried to fix his problem. Yet all attempts to change her son had failed miserably. Finally, she simply gave up and lived in the empty anguish of believing she is a colossal failure, with no hope, no answers, and no support from anyone.

Prodigals need love, but we give them shame. They need understanding, yet we give them demands. If something is going to change, it must begin with us as parents, not with the prodigals. Instead of trying so hard to control their circumstances to get them to change, we need to trust God to change us. One of the most important concepts of this book is that most often, it is the parents of prodigals who are most in need of change. As you go through the rest of the book, you will discover six principles to provide guidelines, insight, and encouragement to help you make those needed changes.

> **If something is going to change, it must begin with us as parents, not with the prodigals.**

A CLOSER LOOK . . .

1. What kinds of prodigals are in your life? List them here and describe the characteristics that make them embarrassing, defiant, intellectual, lukewarm, or religious.

2. Have you responded to your prodigal's situation in any of the following ways? If so, describe your attitude and actions here:

— Condemnation

— Self-blame

— Ignoring the problem

— Lies and cover-ups

— Nagging

— Attempts to fix the problem

— Quiet anguish

3. How have you tried to change the prodigals in your life? (Be specific about the words and actions you have used.)

In what ways have these attempts been successful? In what ways have they driven a deeper wedge between you and the prodigal?

PRINCIPLE #1: LEARN TO LIVE GUILT-FREE

"*W*hat did I do wrong?" This haunting question is echoed hundreds of times in conversations I have with parents. It is human nature for us to assign blame. Determining responsibility can be helpful if it leads to forgiveness and healing, but if condemnation is the only outcome, our analysis is destructive.

Some parents are motivated by compassion as they seek a solution and try to help the one they love. If they can unmask the problem, they can address it forcefully and clearly. But far too many parents are consumed with guilt rather than compassion. They believe the long, bony finger of blame points back at them, and they are disillusioned under the tremendous weight of responsibility they feel for their child's problems. Let's look at some truths from God's Word that will help us escape this crushing weight of guilt.

ALL HAVE SINNED

Paul told the Roman believers, "For all have sinned and fall short of the glory of God" (Rom 3:23). Theologians speak of "the depravity of man." This means that we are fallen, sinful people from birth. We don't have to teach people to sin; they do it naturally. We also know from Scripture that we each have freedom of choice.

The Bible is full of instructions and admonitions to guide our choices. Paul typically uses half of each of his letters to the churches to describe the glorious truths about our identity in Christ, and he uses the other half to instruct us how that identity should be expressed in our choices. For example, in his letter to the Ephesians, he first describes how God calls us: we are chosen by God, adopted, loved, and forgiven. Then he turns to application of those truths. "I, therefore, the prisoner of the Lord, beseech you to walk worthy of the calling with which you were called" (Eph 4:1). After this transition to the second half of the letter, he encourages us to follow commands such as: don't lie, but speak the truth; don't steal, but give to those in need; don't be bitter, but forgive; don't destroy people with your words, but speak words that build people up. Obviously, he provides these clear commands because we have such a tendency to lie, steal, harbor bitterness, and use our words to hurt people. We have a propensity to sin, yet we have other choices as well.

Your prodigal has choices, too. When a person becomes an adult, he is responsible for his own behavior:

> **We are often quick to excuse our prodigals' behavior and blame ourselves when they act badly, but even if we had been perfect parents, we couldn't guarantee a child's godliness.**

his choices, his attitudes, and his actions. He may act like a selfish, spoiled child, but God will hold him accountable as an adult. He may have suffered terribly as a child, and his life may be colored by many tragic experiences, but he is still accountable for his own choices. We are often quick to excuse our prodigals' behavior and blame ourselves when they act badly, but even if we had been perfect parents, we couldn't guarantee a child's godliness.

In Jesus' Parable of the Prodigal Son, what sins do we see the father commit? How do we see him alienate his son and drive him away from home? We don't. It's simply not in the story. He was as good a parent as we can find. Still, his son chose to reject his father's company in pursuit of other, less beneficial, options.

The Bible provides several examples of people who made bad choices even after they enjoyed a good environment. Jesus spent three years with His twelve disciples. He never sinned, and He always showed them perfect love, yet Judas betrayed Him for 30 pieces of silver, and the rest of the disciples ran at His moment of greatest need.

Adam and Eve lived in the perfection of the Garden. They had everything they could possibly want, but they chose to sin against God because they were promised even more power to "be like God, knowing good and evil." They got their wish. Before that day, they had never known evil, but from that day on, evil has shadowed every moment for them and their descendents.

The children of Israel were rescued from slavery in Egypt. Miracles marked the beginning of their journey, and miracles sustained them day after day. But they grumbled and complained so often that God let that first generation die in the desert instead of allowing them to enter the Promised Land.

In the early church, Paul discipled a man named Demas. At first, he was a faithful follower who ministered alongside Paul and Luke. In his short letter to Philemon, Paul referred to Demas as "my fellow worker" (Philemon 24). In Paul's eyes, Demas was a valued friend and co-laborer in the cause of Christ, at the same level as Mark, the gospel writer. But in a later letter to Timothy, Paul reported sadly, "For Demas has forsaken me, having loved this present world, and has departed for Thessalonica" (II Tim 4:10). Demas enjoyed the encouragement and the example of the apostle Paul, one of the greatest Christians in all of history, yet he chose to become a prodigal and leave Paul because he longed for comfort and wealth.

Each of these examples depicts someone who was loved and valued deeply, by Jesus personally, by God in the Garden, or by the apostle Paul, but in each case, perfect love failed to keep those people from becoming prodigals. They made their own choices to turn away from God. So the first point I want to make—and make it clearly—is that your prodigal is responsible for his own choices. Even if you had been a perfect parent, which none of us are, that wouldn't have guaranteed that your son or daughter would have chosen to remain strong in Christ.

WHAT DOES PROVERBS 22:6 MEAN, ANYWAY?

One of the most common laments I've heard from parents is, "Doesn't the Bible say that if I'd been a better parent, my child would be walking with the Lord today?" The reference is to Proverbs 22:6, which has been a source of tremendous guilt and confusion for parents of prodigals. I want to clarify what this passage means. It reads:

"Train up a child in the way he should go,
And when he is old he will not depart from it."

Many people look at this verse as a promise rather than a proverb. Promises are always true; proverbs are generally true, but not always. For example, another proverb says that a man who sleeps with harlots will lose his wealth. While it is true that sexual sins often cost people a lot of money, I know some men who regularly visit prostitutes but are still very rich.

> **"Doesn't the Bible say that if I'd been a better parent, my child would be walking with the Lord today?"**

The proverb about training up children has been explained in many ways. Some scholars say it means to instruct a child on his level so he will understand the truth. Others say that the term "in the way he should go" refers to a child's "bent." That is, parents should notice each child's particular gifts, skills, and personality, and give encouragement and direction based on those traits. So a child who is gifted in art could be given lessons in painting and sculpting; a child who is athletically talented should be given opportunities to play sports; and a child who is good at math is encouraged to pursue more challenging course work in algebra and calculus.

This interpretation makes good sense to me, and I think parents are right in observing and nurturing the particular skills of each of their children. Yet as I have studied this passage of Scripture, I believe there is another meaning for us to consider. Psychologists tell us that childhood profoundly shapes our lives. How we are raised affects us for the rest of our lives, for good or ill. If a child is told she is fat and ugly, she will probably be insecure about her appearance as an adult. If a child is abused or neglected, those scars will make him cautious in relationships even after being placed in a safe environment. If a child is constantly nagged and criticized, he will doubt his abilities.

> **Proverbs 22:6 is not a promise that the child will never depart from God's path, but instead it reminds us that God's message remains rooted in that person's life and cannot be eradicated.**

These are the negative aspects we usually tend to focus on, but there is also a positive side to the same principle. If a child is exposed to the ways and the truth of God when he is young, those messages will stay in his heart for the rest of his life. Though his choices and behavior may take him far from God, the truth of God stays lodged in his mind. So Proverbs 22:6 is not a promise that the child will never depart from God's path, but instead it reminds us that God's message remains rooted in that person's life and cannot be eradicated.

Do you remember what happened to the Prodigal Son? He had gone as far away from his father as he could go. He was feeding hogs in a foreign land, penniless and friendless, but even there he remembered his father's goodness and strength. The childhood memories of his father's love prompted a desire to return to his dad as he realized he might be extended the grace to repent and come home.

Dr. Earl Radmacher, a Bible scholar and former seminary president, comments on this verse:

> "Some have taken the line 'when he is old he will not depart from it' as a promise. They believe it to be a guarantee that proper parenting will always result in a child's salvation. Proverbs, however, present general principles, not promises. This verse gives parents the assurance that the lessons learned in childhood will last a lifetime. Whether their child learns to follow the Lord will, in part, depend on his or her own choices. But the lessons driven home at the crucial stage of childhood will not go away."[2]

Nowhere in Scripture does it say that if you had just done the right thing as a parent, your child would be walking with God today. No, the Scriptures teach two important lessons: (1) Each person has a free will and a sinful nature, and (2) If your child was exposed to the word of God, that truth is still there to be tapped by the

2 *The Nelson Study Bible,* Earl D. Radmacher, Th.D, General Editor (Thomas Nelson Publishers, Nashville, 1997), p. 1064.

Holy Spirit whenever your child "comes to his senses." These two lessons help us clarify responsibility so we can be relieved of guilt.

> Our human nature demands that somebody take the blame when things go wrong. Many times, we turn our guns on ourselves. Other times we blast away at somebody—anybody!—else.

THE BLAME GAME

Our human nature demands that somebody take the blame when things go wrong. Many times, we turn our guns on ourselves. Other times we blast away at somebody—anybody!—else. I've heard parents blame a youth pastor for their child's waywardness. "If he had just called one more time, Roy would have gone to church camp that summer instead of starting to smoke marijuana and eventually becoming a drug addict." Doesn't this reasoning sound far-fetched? Yet I've heard many parents do mental and emotional gymnastics in order to place blame on somebody or some situation. One lady told me, "Judy's biology teacher spent so much time talking about reproduction, I just know that's what got Judy interested in sex. She got pregnant, and it's that biology teacher's fault." (As if Judy wouldn't have been interested in sex if she hadn't learned about the reproductive habits of frogs!)

I've also heard parents desperately search for a circumstance in the past that will magically explain why their child has become a prodigal. A lady explained solemnly, "My son and his best friend were riding their bikes when they were nine years old. A car hit Jeff's friend, and he almost died as result. I just know Jeff has never been the same since then. He became an alcoholic and has gone through four divorces, but it all goes back to that day when his best friend got run over."

Sometimes, of course, the blame is more rational. An elderly gentleman told me that his son had been molested by their assistant pastor many years before. "My boy's not in church today," he related sadly. "I'm sure that terrible experience is what drove him away from church." While I agree that being molested by a pastor would have very negative effects on a young man, I also know people who have been victims of sexual abuse and every other kind of terrible interpersonal sin who have experienced healing, hope, and a new relationship with God. As adults, we are all responsible for our choices, even our responses to being victimized by others.

COMPARISON KILLS

Many parents are proud of their children, and rightly so. They love to tell everyone who will listen about their son's successful business or their daughter's mission experience. However, when parents of prodigals hear these stories, it is like salt has been poured in their wounds. Instead of being encouraged, they feel self-doubt and discouragement all over again. And their pain seems more severe when contrasted to someone else's joy. The prodigal's parent hears words that aren't actually spoken, but scream nonetheless. Any happy, proud parent seems to rebuke them: "If you were as spiritual as I am, your child would be doing well, too."

As a result, parents of prodigals play the "if only" game. They speculate:

- "If only I'd had a better job like Sam Johnson, then I would have made enough so my Mary could have gone to a better school and not gotten into trouble."
- "If only my husband hadn't died. My son needed a stronger hand to guide him."
- "If only we'd taken more time for vacations, my kids would care about us more now that we're older."
- "If only we'd gone to a different church, my son would have gotten better teaching about walking with God. His life would be different today."

Parents can think of a thousand "if only's" and "what if's," but none of them soothe the pain. Such thoughts only redirect the blame to themselves and never offer any remedy. The past cannot be changed now, so the parent is left feeling more ashamed, more guilty, and more hopeless.

I GUESS I'LL JUST HIDE

Guilt can crush us from inside, sapping the joy out of life and leaving us lonely, bitter, and discouraged. Many parents have lived with guilt so long that they have adopted three "rules" of painful families: Don't talk, don't trust, and don't feel.

They converse about everything and anything, except the pain they feel. They may even ask for prayer for their prodigal. But when somebody asks, "How are you doing with all this?" they smile sweetly and say, "Oh, I'm fine. Don't worry about me." They are dying inside, but don't want anybody to know it.

Parents who have been repeatedly disappointed grow disillusioned and give up on having a meaningful relationship, one based on trust, with their wayward sons or daughters. Instead, they talk only about surface things and avoid mention of topics that are painful—or important. Disappointment also colors the parents' relationships with God. They have hoped so long and prayed so hard, but God hasn't changed their prodigals' hearts. Their trust in God has vanished, and they stop seeking meaning and joy. Instead, their goal becomes avoiding any more pain.

The disillusioned parents enter a world of numbness where hurts are not as intense, but neither is joy. If they don't find some relief, depression sets in—sometimes mind- and body-numbing clinical depression. This condition may occur gradually, but usually a traumatic and explosive fight with the prodigal sends parents "over the edge" into emotional despair and darkness. Things that used to make them happy become tedious. Friends become a nuisance. They either sleep too much or not at all. Eating seems like too much trouble, or they eat constantly.

> **Their trust in God has vanished, and they stop seeking meaning and joy. Instead, their goal becomes avoiding any more pain.**

Don't talk, don't trust, don't feel. These sinister "rules" become the norm for parents of prodigals if they don't relieve their guilt with peace, forgiveness, and joy.

PERSONAL RESPONSIBILITY

Many parents want to blame other people for their prodigals' problems, and viciously condemn those they feel are at fault. Yet even the most vocal among them usually realize that at some point they contributed to the problem in a significant way. Perhaps they nagged too much, or maybe they were working so hard they weren't around when they were needed. Maybe they were overprotective and didn't allow their kids to make their own decisions, and now those children have made an important and painful decision: to stay away from their oppressive parents.

Every parent I know remembers and regrets certain actions in the past: yelling at their children without reason, spanking them too hard, or some other offense. We all make mistakes. The problem occurs when we refuse to say, "I was wrong. Please forgive me."

If we are listening, God uses our consciences to show us our faults. But just because God tweaks our conscience doesn't mean He is piling on condemnation. The Bible describes a huge difference between oppressive guilt and the conviction of the Holy Spirit. Conviction is the process of God getting me to acknowledge my sin in order to confess, be forgiven, and put it behind me. Guilt simply makes me feel bad for what I've done. Conviction is forward thinking; guilt is backward thinking. Guilt is accompanied by an inability to accept God's will, God's provision, and God's forgiveness. Guilt makes us feel that if we punish ourselves severely enough and long enough, we can compensate for our faults.

One time Paul discovered that the Corinthian believers were committing serious sins, so he wrote them a letter to challenge them to repent. To his delight, they responded to his instructions. When he learned of their response, he wrote:

> "For though I made you sorry with my letter, I do not regret it; though I did regret it. For I perceive that the same epistle made you sorry, though only for a while. Now I rejoice, not that you were made sorry, but that your sorrow led to repentance. For you were made sorry in a godly manner, that you might suffer loss from us in nothing. For godly sorrow produces repentance to salvation, not to be regretted; but the sorrow of the world produces death" (II Cor 7:8-10).

"The sorrow of the world produces death." That's guilt. The death Paul is talking about is the sense that we are helpless, hopeless, and worthless, without God and without remedy to solve our problems. But in contrast, "godly sorrow produces repentance . . . not to be regretted" —that's the conviction of the Holy Spirit.

When we experience God's cleansing grace for our sins, we are thankful to be forgiven. Paul said it another way in his letter to the Romans: "There is therefore now

> **There is no condemnation any more, only forgiveness. No more oppressive guilt, only grace.**

no condemnation to those who are in Christ Jesus" (Rom 8:1). If you and I have trusted Christ as Savior, His grace covers all our sins, even those which have hurt those we value most dearly. There is no condemnation any more, only forgiveness. No more oppressive guilt, only grace.

Let me outline some of the differences between destructive guilt and the positive conviction of the Holy Spirit. It's guilt if:

- It tells us we are condemned and unworthy. What we have done is so bad that nothing can ever overcome it.
- It makes us want to hide.
- It focuses on others' opinions of us.
- It produces fear.
- It makes us want to find someone else to blame.

In contrast, it's probably the conviction of the Holy Spirit if:

- It tells us our behavior is wrong, but that we are still loved by God.
- It gives us courage to approach those we have hurt to restore the relationship.
- It focuses on God's opinion of us. We want to please Him above all else.
- It produces joy.
- It leads to repentance, forgiveness, and refreshment so we don't feel compelled to blame anyone anymore.

We must use both reason and faith to move beyond any oppressive guilt we feel to experience the joy of being forgiven and loved by God. Don't interpret your prodigal's behavior as an indictment of you. Others may believe that lie, but God doesn't. You undoubtedly did the best you knew how to do. If you wronged your child, as we all have in one way or another, respond to the conviction of God's Spirit and experience His refreshing grace.

FINDING GRACE IN STRANGE PLACES

Recently, a couple in their mid-70's asked to talk to me after I spoke at their church. Their daughter had been recently divorced and remarried, and they had misgivings about her new husband. She had retained custody of her five-year-old daughter. The young girl had called, sounding troubled and asking to visit her grandparents. When she arrived, she was barely in the front door when she blurted out that her mother and new stepfather were dealing drugs.

The grandfather asked a few questions and found out more than he bargained for. The young girl told him detailed facts about her parents' client list and suppliers. Her stepfather had a minimum wage job, but he was driving a Jaguar and booking reservations on a cruise. All that money had to be coming from somewhere.

The grandparents feared for their daughter's life, but even more, they were concerned for their granddaughter's safety. They had seen enough reports on the local news to know that drug dealers were put in jail, or worse, were sometimes killed when a drug deal went bad. They went to a counselor for advice, and he immediately advised them to go to the authorities. If they went to the authorities, they believed, they could plead for mercy.

At the police station, the grandfather learned that his son-in-law was already under surveillance. The police said they needed further information before they could arrest the couple. The grandfather went back home, got additional details from the little girl, and took the information to the police department. The police then arrested his daughter and son-in-law, and they went to prison.

During the trial, the couple found out that her parents turned them in. They were irate and hired a lawyer to prevent the grandparents from seeing the little girl. Even though the parents went to jail, the court decided the grandparents could see their granddaughter only once a month for two hours.

The grandfather told me, "Phil, I wish I'd never gone to the police. Ten thousand times I'd take it back. Now my daughter and son-in-law have nothing to do with me. They say they're going to kill us when they get out. I can only see my granddaughter for two hours a month now, and they say when they get out I'll never see her again. She will be a teenager then. I feel just awful because I didn't do the right thing."

The old gentleman's wife cried as he told their story, yet through her tears she told me confidently, "Phil, I came to the conclusion that we did the right thing. I don't have guilt, because I have faith that when my granddaughter listens to the whole story, she'll know we acted in her best interests. I came to the conclusion, as painful as it is, that sometimes doing the right thing costs a lot."

This couple exemplifies two responses to a prodigal. The man felt guilt because he couldn't make his daughter walk with God, and he couldn't get her to treat him with even a little respect. He was crushed. His wife, on the other hand, was a paragon of insight, grace, and strength. She refused to believe her daughter's lies and accusations. Instead, she held tightly to the truth

> **She was deeply grieved over what had happened, but her grief didn't cloud the truth. She is an example for any parent of a prodigal.**

and trusted that God would someday, somehow, make it all right. She was deeply grieved over what had happened, but her grief didn't cloud the truth. She is an example for any parent of a prodigal.

A CLOSER LOOK . . .

1. Have you felt guilty because you couldn't get your prodigal to turn back to God? Explain how you have felt about yourself and what you have done to try to overcome your guilt.

2. How does it help you to know that your prodigal is responsible for his own choices?

3. How does the explanation of Proverbs 22:6 in this chapter give you fresh insight about your responsibility and hope that your prodigal may someday "come to his senses"?

4. In what ways have you felt that "somebody has to take the blame"? Who have you blamed for your prodigal's problems?

5. Describe some of your feelings about guilt and conviction. Review this chapter, and then answer these questions:

What does guilt feel like?

What does conviction feel like?

How can you tell the difference?

6. Describe some of the differences between guilt and conviction (the motivations, the goals, the effects on you and on your relationships, etc.).

7. Take a few minutes to respond to the Holy Spirit's prompting. If you sense He is showing you any ways you have sinned against your prodigal, take this opportunity to confess the sin and experience God's cleansing grace.

🔷

PRINCIPLE #2: ASK FOR FORGIVENESS

Some of us know exactly how we've hurt our children. We had an affair and walked out. We lost control and slapped them. We weren't there when they needed us. We yelled, "I wish you were never born!" Those memories remain just as harsh to us as they are to our children.

Others of us aren't sure what the problem is. Something went wrong for sure, but we don't have any idea what it is. Our relationship with one child may be just fine, but with the prodigal there is coolness and distance.

A man recently told me about his grown, married son who has always been cool toward him, yet has a close and personal relationship with his in-laws. The man first noticed a strain in the relationship when his son was in high school, but he discounted it as a phase. When the young man went to college, he came home only sporadically, and then his times with his father were pleasant but superficial. When the father asked personal questions, his son gave quick answers and changed the subject. Clearly, he didn't want his father to know his heart.

The father tried to rationalize this distance in their relationship, but as time went on, rationalization gradually gave way to heartache. After his son got married, he noticed how free and relaxed his son seemed to be with his in-laws, and the pain cut like a knife. But he said nothing. He felt he must have done something to hurt his son, but he didn't want to bring up old wounds. After all, they weren't arguing and cursing each other. Their relationship, he assured himself, was far better than that of a lot of fathers and sons.

> ...And the pain cut like a knife. But he said nothing. He felt he must have done something to hurt his son, but he didn't want to bring up old wounds.

But after several more years, the pain had become unbearable. I suggested that he ask his son if there was anything that had caused the problem. At first, he protested, "If I did anything to hurt him, surely he would have said something by now, Phil. It's been years!"

"Or he may be wondering why you haven't said anything after all these years," I answered him.

This sad father nodded and said he would give it a try. He was willing to do anything to resolve the hurt he felt. When his son and family visited the next summer, he asked his son to join him on the back porch. There, he swallowed hard and said, "Son, this is hard for me. It seems there has been distance between us for some time. I can't think of any childhood event that would have hurt you, but there must be something. Please tell me what I've done to offend you."

The son took a deep breath. Tears welled up in his eyes, and he told his dad, "Yes, sir. You hurt me deeply when I was 13. Do you remember when I made the All-Star baseball team that summer?"

His father nodded, "Yes, I was really proud of you."

"You were out of town for our first playoff game. I called and told you, 'Dad, we won! The championship game is Friday night. You'll be there, won't you?' But you said you couldn't make it."

His father began to speak, but the son waved him off. "Dad, that's not what hurt. But the next week Charles [his dad's favorite nephew] called and asked you to go to his game. Dad, you took a day of vacation to go to his game, but you didn't go to mine. That's what really hurt." Tears were flowing down the son's cheeks.

This dad had been a surrogate father to his nephew because his sister was a single mom. He could have explained that Charles needed as much affirmation as possible and that he had spent plenty of quality time with his own son. He had a good excuse, but he didn't say those things. Instead of defending himself, he replied, "Son, I am so sorry. Please forgive me. Thank you so much for talking to me."

If the dad had defended himself, even justifiably, the son would have walked away with an even deeper wound. But this wise man didn't try to explain his behavior at all. He just apologized. That day marked a turning point in their relationship. The coolness gave way to warmth, and superficial conversation turned into deep, heart-felt communication. The father's only regret was that he hadn't talked to his son twenty years earlier. All those years of distance and tension could have been cut short by one honest conversation, but excuses, rationalization, and fear stood in the way.

Forgiveness is the cornerstone of our relationship with God, and it ought to be the cornerstone of our human relationships as well. In fact, honesty with God about our sinfulness is a springboard for honesty in our other relationships. Those simple words, "I was wrong. Please forgive me," are incredibly powerful. They open doors of truth and grace in our relationships with those we love. Far too often, however, we are too proud to utter them.

TYPES OF WOUNDS

When we think of sinning against our children, our thoughts may drift to the extreme examples we hear about on the evening news: "A mother locked her two children in the trunk of her car when she went shopping. One died and the other is in intensive care." Or, "A father killed his wife and children in a drunken rage. Detectives are still trying to determine his motives." These and similar stories horrify us, but few of us have committed such terrible acts. Most of our offenses won't make the evening news. They are common, and that fact makes them harder to identify and resolve. I would classify the types of hurts we inflict as: (1) Shattering wounds, (2) Eroding wounds, and (3) Vacuum wounds.

Shattering wounds

Physical or sexual abuse shatters a child's heart and leaves him or her broken, inside and out. Other traumatic experiences also are sledgehammers on a child's soul: the sudden and/or violent death of a parent, witnessing one parent physically abusing the other, and so forth. One parent tried to excuse himself by saying, "Well, I didn't do it that often." But it doesn't take many traumatic experiences to create deep and permanent wounds.

> **But it doesn't take many traumatic experiences to create deep and permanent wounds.**

Eroding wounds

More common are the sandpaper effects of harsh, condemning messages. "You'll never amount to anything!" "Can't you do anything right?" "Why don't you get out of here and leave me alone?" Comparison to others can be just as destructive, as when a distraught parent barks, "Why can't you be like your sister?"

Some of these messages are overcome with lots of love and repentance. But where there is no repentance, the wound stays unhealed and festers. In many cases, the parents tell themselves, "At least I didn't beat her. She needed come correction, and I gave it to her." But these parents gave precious little love and affirmation along with their correction. The result was harsh condemnation and shattered self-confidence.

Janice was 11 years old when her mother fell in love with another man and decided to leave her husband.

> **But these parents gave precious little love and affirmation along with their correction. The result was harsh condemnation and shattered self-confidence.**

Janice overheard her mother tell a neighbor, "I don't want my kids. I don't care if I never see them again!" She moved out, planning to disappear without a trace.

A few days later, however, Janice's mother found out that her lover refused to leave his wife and marry her. In the aftermath of this event, God touched this mother's heart and she became a Christian. She came back home and was reconciled to her husband. But when Janice reminded her mother of the penetrating, damaging words she had overheard, her mother didn't want to talk about it. She quickly told Janice, "Oh, you know I was just kidding."

Janice's mother never apologized for saying she didn't want the children. In fact, the family swept that episode under the rug and never discussed it. Her father once told Janice, "I've forgiven your mother for having an affair and leaving. Now she's home, and everything's the way it should be. We don't need to discuss it again."

But Janice retained a deep and painful emotional wound. The initial trauma gave way to the erosion caused by repeated messages that she wasn't important enough to warrant addressing the issue. When Janice was asked about it years later as an adult, she replied tartly, "I know how my mother feels about me." She completely detached from her mother and maintains a very superficial relationship with the family.

In recent years, her mother has tried to reach out to her, yet still refuses to talk with Janice about the event that caused such pain. The last time Janice brought it up, her mother cut her off quickly with the comment, "That's ancient history, Janice. We need to live in the present. Just let it go." Janice walked out, hurt again that her mother was unwilling to even acknowledge her pain. After this brief exchange, her mother explained to her dad, "I didn't mean what I said that day. And besides, she was eavesdropping. I wouldn't have said it if I'd known she was listening. I wish she'd just drop it and get on with her life."

Janet experienced this tragic crisis at an age when little girls are close to their mothers. At that vulnerable moment in her life, she was deeply wounded. She still is. A whole world of healing and hope might open up if this mother, who is now a Christian, would acknowledge that what she did was wrong and ask for Janice's forgiveness.

Vacuum wounds

One of the wounds hardest to heal is neglect. Physical abuse leaves bruises. With verbal abuse, we associate harsh words and scowling faces, but we can experience an entire childhood of neglect without having a distinctive wound to identify or an

> **We can experience an entire childhood of neglect without having a distinctive wound to identify or an evident loss to grieve—only emptiness.**

evident loss to grieve—only emptiness. Yet after talking to hundreds of young people over the years, I believe neglect is one of the most painful and difficult wounds in the world.

Men, especially those who grew up before the current trend of male sensitivity, often appear unfazed by the pain of others. They learned to "suck it up" when they felt hurt, so they expect their children to do the same thing. Vince Lombardi is one of their heroes. The legendary coach of the Green Bay Packers was a man's man, a motivator, and someone who produced champions. He was tough, and he didn't coddle his players. At one point, one of them blew out his ACL (a ligament in the knee) and was writhing on the field in pain. Lombardi walked over to him and barked, "Get up and get back in the game! You're not hurt!" I've talked to some grown prodigals who feel this hardhearted sentiment is a perfect description of their fathers' lack of compassion when they were hurting.

Spiritual wounds

One of the most painful and confusing experiences a child can undergo has been labeled "toxic faith." When physical and verbal offenses occur in a home, the child always feels helpless. But when they take place in a home that professes to follow Christ, and especially if the offenses are committed in the name of Christ, the child also feels terrified or angry at God—and utterly hopeless.

I've known people who wouldn't darken the door of a church because their deacon father was so mean to them. One woman told me she was viciously spanked if she failed to perfectly memorize the Bible verses her mother assigned to her. In most of these cases, the parents have reputations in the community as paragons of Christian virtue, so the children are terrified of exposing the lie and incurring even more wrath. They feel trapped. They can't turn to their parents for truth and comfort, and they are afraid of God as well.

Jill, a woman in her 40's, told me that her father was a leader in their church. He taught Sunday school and served on several committees and boards. People in the church and in the community saw him as a respected, godly leader. Jill revered her father, but she felt little love from him. She told me, "What my father said was the law around our house. He wouldn't tolerate any questions of his authority. None at all. He read the Bible to us every night, but it seemed he loved the Old Testament best—you know, the stories about wars and God's judgment on the people when they were disobedient. I can't remember him laughing and smiling around the house, and I can't remember him hugging me. When I was a little girl, I was terrified of him. I loved him dearly—all little girls love their fathers—but I was so afraid of him. When I became a teenager, I was like any other adolescent. I wanted to wear the latest clothes and new hairstyles and hang out with friends, but Dad would have nothing of it. He told me I was being worldly, and he warned that I would go to hell if I didn't do what he said. I wish I had a nickel for every time he quoted Exodus 20:12: 'Honor your father and your mother, that your days may be long upon the land which the Lord your God is giving you.' It got to where I couldn't stand it any more. One night I went out drinking with some friends, and when I got home, you'd have thought I had worshiped Satan or something. Dad came unglued! He told me I had sinned against God and against him, and he was ashamed of me. He didn't speak to me for a month after that. And when he did start speaking to me again, I wish he hadn't."

I asked her, "Jill, where was your mother during all this?"

> **"What relationship with God? I was just as terrified of God as I was of my father..."**

"Oh, she was right there," Jill's eyes widened. "She saw it all, but she was just as terrified of him as I was. Sometimes, when Dad was really angry at me, she'd come in my room and say something like, 'Jill, it would be a lot easier around here if you'd just do what your father says. He'd be a lot happier.' I never saw my mother stand up to him. Not once."

"How did your relationship with your father affect your walk with God?" I probed.

"What relationship with God? I was just as terrified of God as I was of my father. I believed God was good and kind to other people, but I couldn't believe He loved me—not after all the verses about judgment my father quoted over and over again. And not after the way he treated me and my mother."

Jill thought for a moment, then she continued. "It's been only in the last couple of years that I've begun to believe that God might actually love me. I've had a lot of healing to do, but gradually, with the help of some friends, it's happening. My Dad is still just as distant and judgmental as he used to be, but I don't listen to him like I did when I was young. I still love my Dad. I really do. But unless God does something drastic in his life, I know that this is the best relationship we're going to have. It's not much, but it's all he's willing to have. I'm certainly willing to take steps forward, and I've tried to talk to him about the way I feel, but he won't talk about it. It's like I'm speaking a foreign language or something. At least I can see that I'm a lot more loving toward my daughter than he was toward me."

Jesus came, John's gospel tells us, "full of grace and truth." Children, and all the rest of us, need truth. But we need grace just as much. It's not one or the other. Some parents have meant well by giving their children rigid religious demands and harsh punishments justified (they believe) by Scripture, but use of "the rod" needs to be coupled with kindness, understanding, and lots of love and forgiveness.

THE REAL THING

The concept of forgiveness is found throughout the pages of Scripture. In the Old Testament, the children of Israel were instructed to follow elaborate Temple rituals, including blood sacrifices for sins. They looked forward to a day when a perfect sacrifice would come. And He did. Jesus' death on the cross was the fulfillment of the Old Testament prophecies about the coming Messiah. Jesus was the "Lamb of God," who, as His cousin John the Baptist, said, would "take away the sins of the world."

During His earthly ministry, Jesus taught and modeled forgiveness for His followers. Matthew 18 includes a parable about an unforgiving servant. This servant owed the king "ten thousand talents." A talent was a unit of measurement, 20 to 50 pounds of a precious metal, usually silver or gold. In today's valuation of gold, the servant owed the king almost two billion dollars! Jesus obviously wanted to emphasize that this was an amount far more than the servant could ever hope to repay. Ordinarily, the debtor and his family would be forced to become indentured servants until the debt was repaid (in this case, for the rest of their lives). The king, however, felt compassion for the servant and released him from the debt. That was wonderful news, but it wasn't the end of the story.

The servant had loaned a fellow servant a comparatively paltry amount of money. But when the second servant couldn't repay his debt, the forgiven servant choked him and threw him into prison. Other servants told the king what the first servant had done, and the king was furious. The experience of forgiveness should have made a difference in the man's life. It should have made him more thankful and compassionate, but he failed to learn that lesson. Consequently, the king "was angry and delivered him to the torturers until he should pay all that was due him" (Matt 18:34). Jesus didn't want the point to be lost on His hearers. He explained that they must let God's forgiveness sink deep into their souls so it shaped their relationships. He told them, "So My heavenly Father also will do to you if each of you, from his heart,

does not forgive his brother his tres-
passes" (vs 35).

Giving and receiving forgiveness
on the human level requires a depth
of experience of God's forgiveness of
us. If we have drunk deeply of God's
great grace and felt the cleansing
flood of His forgiveness, we can be
more honest about our own sins and
more compassionate toward those
who sin against us. If, however, we
fail to drink deeply of God's grace,
we become defensive and angry
people. Many of us feel tortured by
the hurt and anger we have experienced in our most precious and dear
relationships. We need the courage to
be honest—with God, with ourselves,
and with our loved ones.

> **If we have drunk deeply of God's great grace and felt the cleansing flood of His forgiveness, we can be more honest about our own sins and more compassionate toward those who sin against us.**

In an article in *Christianity Today* many years ago,
popular author Philip Yancey wrote an article entitled
"The Unnatural Act." The article said that people want
justice to punish an offender far more than they want to
forgive him. Forgiveness, therefore, is "unnatural." In the
same way, asking for forgiveness is also "unnatural." We
would much rather retreat or talk about something else
than to admit that we are wrong and have hurt someone.
Facing those we offended and confessing our faults takes
great courage, but it is the vital step in reconciliation.

EXPLAINING DOESN'T WORK

Many senior adults only want to seek forgiveness when they are absolutely sure they were wrong, and even then, they are very hesitant. They often say, "I'm not going to ask him to forgive me. I've done nothing wrong."

I've witnessed arguments in families when the mother tries to play the peacemaker. The child says her father didn't pay enough attention to her, but the father refuses to admit it. The mother jumps in the middle and says to her husband, "Well, honey, you *did* work two jobs when Alice was little, so she *might* have felt neglected."

He grumbles, "Yeah, but she doesn't appreciate all I did for her."

Then the mom pleads with her daughter, "Dear, he was doing all that for you. Please don't be angry."

Nothing gets resolved. In fact, the daughter feels even more alienated from her father because he refused to even try to understand her feelings and her perspective. While the father makes excuses and the mother tries to make treaties, the daughter continues to hurt. Explaining and excusing are no substitutes for forgiveness.

> **Explaining and excusing are no substitutes for forgiveness.**

Many prodigals tell me, "When I was growing up, my dad worked seven days a week, 10 hours a day. Dad didn't have time for my ball games or piano recitals." Parents accused of neglecting their children because they worked so hard almost invariably reply, "But you don't understand. I grew up during the Depression and World War II.

We often went to bed hungry. I didn't have books to read. I cried because I didn't have toys to play with, and I vowed that my children would never suffer like I did." This determination led them to work long hours to be sure their children didn't go hungry. The problem was that these children went hungry for love.

Thirty or forty years ago, before Dr. Spock, parents challenged children to be better and do more. If a boy came home from school with straight A's, a parent might remark, "That's pretty good," but would follow up with a sly smile, "I bet you can't do it again." The parent wanted the child to feel motivated to keep trying hard. If the child felt the remark was condemning instead, the parent would explain, "I'm challenging him to be the best he can be." But what too many youngsters believed was, "I can never do enough to please my parents." The parents wanted to help the child excel, but the child felt only a sense of disappointing them.

TAKE THE INITIATIVE

Most parents I know wait as long as possible before talking to their prodigals about the strain in their relationship. Most go for years abiding by an unspoken truce, with long periods of tension-filled non-belligerence occasionally punctuated by open attacks and vicious reprisals. Some have told me, "If there was something wrong, she'd tell me. I don't want to stir up something that isn't there." So another year—or another decade—passes with no resolution. The bursts of anger are quickly swept under the rug instead of being seen for what they are:

> **Don't wait for your prodigal to take the first step. Take it yourself.**

red flags that something is seriously wrong and needs attention.

Don't wait for your prodigal to take the first step. Take it yourself. But be sure you have thought and prayed through it first. Below are some principles to prepare you to say those wonderful words, "Please forgive me."

Ask God for wisdom.

At the close of one of the most beautiful and penetrating psalms, King David asked God to show him any and every fault in his life. He didn't want anything to come between him and God's will for his life. He wanted God to point out any shortcomings so he could be cleansed of his sin and move on in God's great grace. David wrote:

"Search me, O God, and know my heart.
Try me, and know my anxieties;
And see if there is any wicked way in me,
And lead me in the way everlasting"
(Psalm 139:23-24).

Your prodigal's response to you, as well as your own conscience, probably lets you know when you have caused some offense. Like David, ask for insight and trust the Lord to provide wisdom. Ask God to remind you of events in the past that may have hurt your son or daughter, and then be silent and listen. Let the Holy Spirit bring memories to mind. You may be surprised by what He reveals. If you still don't know what you did to hurt your prodigal, ask God to give you wisdom for how to open the conversation so you can ask your prodigal what's wrong and begin the process of reconciliation.

Prepare your opening statement and question.

If you know what you did to hurt your prodigal, you can begin by saying, "Son, there's something very important I want to talk to you about. I've been thinking about that time when you were in junior high and I slapped you [or whatever it was]. That was wrong of me. I am so sorry. Will you please forgive me?" Be honest and straightforward. Don't defend, explain, or excuse yourself in any way. Take responsibility for your actions. No matter how much strain you were under at the time, you are responsible for your actions. If you were wrong, admit it. And don't stop with saying you are sorry. Take the next step and ask for forgiveness.

Anticipate your prodigal's response.

You are taking a different approach that may catch your prodigal off guard. She may weep and thank you for your confession, or she may take this opportunity to yell at you and tell you 473 other things you did that hurt her. Or she may say, "Oh, it was no big deal."

If you have spent years justifying your behavior, denying it, or minimizing the damage it caused, your prodigal has probably done the same thing. Your goal is not to make her respond a certain way. Simply speak the truth and share your heart, then let her respond any way she chooses. Don't be surprised if she has great difficulty accepting your confession. Perhaps in a few days you can talk again. After she's had time to think about it, she may be more willing to absorb the impact of your message and respond accordingly.

Anticipate your response.

How do you normally respond in tense situations? Some of us wither under stress. When someone criticizes us, our brains turn to mush and our legs become jelly. We can't think and we can't act.

Craig had a very honest and painful conversation with his prodigal brother. During the conversation, Craig's brother accused him of all manner of things he had never done. Craig felt attacked. After a few minutes of his brother's barrage, he started slumping down in his chair and becoming part of the carpet! But he noticed what was happening, sat up, strengthened his voice and his message, and reentered the conversation to address the truth.

Some of us respond in the opposite way. When we feel attacked or out of control, we take charge. We talk loudly, we give orders, we demand compliance, and we intimidate people so they will give in to us. But if you're trying to tell your prodigal you have sinned against him and then react in anger if he doesn't immediately respond as you wish, you only add another layer of pain. Know yourself. Anticipate any inappropriate reactions, and compensate for them. In this case, make your confession, ask for forgiveness, and shut your mouth.

> **Forgiving and being forgiven means we won't bring up the offense again and again to the one we've forgiven, or to anyone else.**

Forgiving and being forgiven means we won't bring up the offense again and again to the one we've forgiven, or to anyone else. When God forgives, He removes our transgressions from us "as far as the east is from the west" (Ps 103:12). Satan wants to dredge up every sin we've ever committed, or at least the really bad ones, so he can keep us locked in guilt. But God never reminds us of forgiven sins. He has cleared them out of the way, and He never uses the past to make us feel guilty.

Some of us have reminded our prodigals over and over again of things they've done wrong. Our hope is that the shame will force them to make better decisions, but instead it hurts them deeply. The Prodigal Son's father didn't bring up his son's sins. He never mentioned them. When you forgive your prodigal, follow that example. Don't bring them up again.

In many families, the husband and the wife are on opposite ends of the spectrum in their responses to stress: one withers and the other intimidates. They have operated that way through difficulties in their own relationship, and they perform the same dance with their prodigal. Both need to understand their normal reactions and make specific plans to respond more appropriately. One needs to speak out more boldly and clearly, and the other needs to speak less and listen more intently.

End the conversation with grace.

Initiating a frank discussion with your prodigal does not immediately resolve longstanding problems, but it is a major step in the right direction. Don't expect or demand that the person embrace every word you say and comprehend each detail you share. This dialog merely opens the door for future conversations so the restoration of trust can continue. But this conversation is incredibly important. No longer will the prodigal feel he is solely to blame for the rift between you. When you take responsibility for your actions, he can more easily take responsibility for his.

Make sure you don't get into an argument about the past and who said what to whom. If your prodigal wants to argue, try to diffuse the tension by saying something like, "I really don't know about that. I didn't bring this up to blame anybody. All I want to do is tell you I'm really sorry for what I did and to ask you to forgive me." Arguing may have become a family sport, but you need to replace it with love and understanding if you want to see permanent improvements in your relationships.

MAYBE YOUR PRODIGAL HAS ALREADY TAKEN THE INITIATIVE

I've spoken with prodigals who have told me sadly, "I've tried to talk to Mom and Dad several times. I know they are really mad at me, but they just won't listen to my side of things." Your prodigal may have tried to mend fences in the past. Perhaps she didn't say what you wanted to hear. Maybe she said you were just as much at fault as she was. Maybe she blamed you entirely. But if she has tried to take initiative in the past and has been verbally attacked or ignored, she may be reluctant to try again.

One man told me he tried to talk to his mother about how she had hurt him. His father was an alcoholic, but his deepest hurts came from his mother. She was furious that her husband was out of control, but she took much of her rage out on her three sons. Jacob is the middle of the three boys. When he was in his forties, he lived far away from his childhood home. God brought a lot of healing in his life through his church. His father had died a few years before, and he wanted to try to mend the relationship with his mother. He talked to his pastor to be sure he was saying the right things in the right ways.

Jacob first wrote out exactly what he wanted to say, and then phoned his mother. He told her he wanted to talk about some things that had hindered their relationship, and she grudgingly agreed to listen. He had always given in to her rage before and absorbed all the blame, but this time he was determined to speak the truth. He recalled some of his memories of times when she had been enraged about his dad wasting all their income on whiskey and foolish spending, but had turned her verbal guns on the three sons instead of confronting her husband. Jacob told her how those experiences had hurt him deeply. She tried to interrupt a few times as he spoke, but he told her, "Mother, please let me finish."

Overlook the poor strategy and look into his heart. Find enough love and forgiveness to take the next step yourself.

When he was done, he waited for her reaction. She told him, "Well, Jacob, I don't know what you're talking about. None of those things ever happened."

"None of them?" he asked incredulously.

"Not a one. I'm not sure what you've been reading or who you've been talking to, but you grew up in a wonderful, loving home. Nothing like those things ever took place. Never."

His mother's reaction killed the flickering hope for an honest, loving relationship. Jacob had mustered the courage to be honest. Maybe he could have said things better, but that's not the point. He had taken the bold, loving step toward reconciliation, but his mother had stomped him down.

If your prodigal has tried to talk to you in the past when you weren't ready to listen, bring that up and apologize for your response. The prodigal may not have gotten all the facts straight or may have blamed you instead of confessing his own sins, but he was probably making his best effort to build a bridge between you. Overlook the poor strategy and look into his heart. Find enough love and forgiveness to take the next step yourself.

REASONS WE DON'T ASK FOR FORGIVENESS

As we have seen, confessing our sins to others, especially to those who have hurt us, requires great courage. It is much easier to continue to blame them and feel justified in our self-pity in the role of victims. Below are some of the most common reasons we fail to ask for forgiveness.

"If we don't talk about it, I'm sure the problem will just go away."

Problems that originate in childhood and endure for decades aren't likely to just disappear. Like an infected wound, they fester and swell until they consume our thoughts and hearts. In the short term, ignoring the problems may seem like a good strategy, but it turns out to be terribly destructive in the long run.

"It's not all my fault."

Many of us have relived past events over and over again. We are haunted by what happened that caused such heartache in our most treasured relationships. We admit we made some mistakes, but so did our prodigals, so we don't want to shoulder all the blame. We see the conflict as an "all or nothing" issue: either we take responsibility for all of the problem, or we don't take responsibility for any of it. In time, we almost inevitably choose the latter.

But rather than seeing the problem as all or nothing, we can instead begin to evaluate our own behavior. We can accept responsibility for our own choices and mistakes, but we don't have to take responsibility for others' behavior.

"I didn't mean to hurt anyone."

Sometimes we say harsh things in a fit of rage, and other times conflicts arise because of a genuine misunderstanding. Maybe we do something to protect one child that makes the other feel neglected and unloved. We didn't mean to hurt anyone, so we excuse ourselves. But such excuses short-circuit forgiveness and maintain distance in the relationship.

"Surely he's over it by now."

We are taught that time heals all wounds. But when you talk to prodigals, you'll discover that much time has passed and their wounds are as fresh as ever. The initial confrontation may have happened so long ago that we can hardly remember the details, but the hurts are just as painful and destructive as they were on the day they happened. Time is no substitute for openness, honesty, confession, and love.

"Surely he's forgotten."

Other times we clearly remember what happened, and we are haunted by it. But our fear of addressing the problem creates a strong hope that our deeply offended child has developed selective amnesia and completely forgotten it. We surmise, "Since he hasn't brought it up in years, I guess he doesn't even remember it happened." That's wishful thinking on our part that does nothing to resolve the rift.

"I'll just do it again."

Many of us are ashamed of our rage, name-calling, and other behaviors we've inflicted on our prodigal, but we don't want to talk about them because we are sure we'll do the same things again. We may have been taught that repentance means we'll never commit the same sins again. But more accurately, it means we will do all we can to prevent the same problems from occurring. Old habits and old beliefs die hard, but that's no reason not to attempt to change. A more realistic approach is to confess immediately each time we sin, and ask our prodigals to pray for us as we trust God to change us.

> **Many of us are ashamed of our rage, name-calling, and other behaviors we've inflicted on our prodigal, but we don't want to talk about them because we are sure we'll do the same things again.**

"I'm angry at him and I won't forgive until he apologizes to me first."

My father served as a soldier in the Korean War. The war, as you know, was never won nor lost. It ended in a stalemate, with a demilitarized zone separating North and South Korea. Today, both sides remain in the same positions they held almost 50 years ago, each with guns ready to blast the other if they make an aggressive step. Many family relationships are similar. We live in an armed truce, prepared for the other side to either apologize or fight to the finish. In the meantime, however, we simply sit back and wait.

"I don't know how he'll respond."

Some of us have tried talking in the past, and it didn't go well. We are afraid to try again because we are sure there will be another war if we bring up the hurts of the past. Even if we shoulder the blame, we are afraid our prodigals will use it to accuse us even more. We aren't sure how they will respond, although we fear the worst.

"If I ask for forgiveness, I'll have to change."

Our prodigals have sinned, and they have hurt us very badly. We feel like victims and soon begin to act that way. We wallow in our pain. We gossip to our friends to get their sympathy. We spend long hours thinking about what we expect to be done to make up for all the wrongs committed against us. But if we confess our part in the strained relationships, we have to give up our comfortable roles as victims. It's much more difficult to take responsibility to speak truth, give grace, and become trustworthy in that difficult relationship. Many of us conclude that it's a lot easier to just stay the way we are.

CONFESSION AND FORGIVENESS ARE UNILATERAL

Underlying many of the previous excuses is the assumption that after we take the initiative in reconciling with our prodigals, they must also confess and repent for our efforts to be of any value. That simply is not true. God has called each of us to walk with Him, even if those around us don't. In the same way, He has called each of us to confess our sins to one another even if others don't respond well at all.

Our success is never defined by the response of others, but only by our obedience to God to do what is right. Paul wrote, "We make it our aim, whether present or absent, to be well-pleasing to Him" (II Cor 5:9). We have an audience of One, the Lord Himself. What God thinks of our efforts is far more important than what our prodigal children think. Jesus calls us to radical discipleship, to follow Him when everyone is looking and when no one is looking, when many others are also following Him and when we seem to be alone in our faith.

Jesus told His followers, "If anyone desires to come after Me, let him deny himself, take up his cross, and follow Me. For whoever desires to save his life will lose it, and whoever loses his life for My sake will find it" (Matt 16:24-25). Some parents reading this chapter are thinking, "I just can't tell my prodigal that I was wrong. It's too painful." Jesus understands our pain, but He instructs us to deny our selfish desires to protect ourselves and remain comfortable. He wants us to take up our cross of obedience, in the big things and in the small, and to follow Him in doing what is right, no matter what the cost.

When we do, He promises that we will find true life. We need to confess our sins to those we have hurt, and seek forgiveness. Stop blaming, and confess. Stop justifying, and be honest. Stop hiding, and take action. None of us can be sure how our prodigals will respond, but we can be very sure how our Lord will respond. He will say, "Well done, good and faithful servant. Enter into the joy of your Master." We can rejoice in His love for us as we await a change in our prodigals.

IF THE PRODIGAL SAYS "NEVER!"

Don't expect instant reconciliation. Occasionally prodigals respond to their parents' confessions with immediate heart-felt confessions of their own, but in most cases, the prodigals need time to process this surprising new development in the relationship. After a few days or a few weeks, they might gladly accept the confession and begin the process of restoration. Other times the prodigals are so embittered that they refuse to budge an inch. Their attitude is, "You hurt me badly, and now you're gonna pay! I'm never letting you off the hook!" If this happens to you, here are some things to remember.

> **Don't expect instant reconciliation.**

Choose to forgive.

Instead of harboring bitterness at your prodigal's hard-heartedness, choose to forgive this offense just as you are choosing to forgive the past hurts he has caused. Forgive as quickly as you can and as fully as you can in order to keep each hurt from turning into resentment and bitterness.

Release your guilt.

All we can do is all we can do. You can't undo the past, but if you are forthright and honest with God and your prodigal about the sins you have committed, you can be free of guilt. Remember, there is no condemnation for those who are in Christ. Absorb His great love and forgiveness. Don't let guilt continue to destroy your life.

Remove obstacles.

Try to remove anything that might inhibit the process of reconciliation. If you have been gossiping, don't do it any more. If you have been lying to protect yourself, stop it. If you have been dishonest or unkind in any way, repent and change your behavior.

Be trustworthy.

In most cases, deeply wounded prodigals are reluctant to forgive because they think it means they have to trust someone who has hurt them. They are waiting for you to prove you are trustworthy, and they will test your sincerity to see if you really want to build a relationship on love and honesty. Earning trust takes time and tenacity. Don't give up because your prodigal insists on seeing genuine change in your life before trusting you. You probably have the same reluctance to trust him until you see genuine, long-lasting change, but you can take the initiative and show him it can be done.

Asking for forgiveness is an act of great faith. It requires preparation, anticipation, and courage. Talk to your pastor, and pray for God's wisdom and leadership as you take this bold step. Don't measure your success by your prodigal's reaction, but know that your faithfulness and obedience are pleasing to God. You never know, you may build a bridge between yourself and your prodigal, and that bridge of love may support the first steps he takes on his road home.

A CLOSER LOOK . . .

1. Take time to pray and ask God to reveal to you the things you've done that have hurt your prodigal. As God brings them to your mind, write them here. (You may want to write in code!)

2. Have you created shattering wounds, eroding wounds, or vacuum wounds? Explain.

3. Review Matthew 18:21-35 and Matthew 16:24-25. In what ways is forgiving your prodigal something you want to do?

In what ways is it something you do out of obedience to God?

4. Consider the elements of preparing to ask for forgiveness. Write your own plan according to these guidelines:

    —Ask God for wisdom.

    —Prepare your opening statement and question.

—Anticipate your prodigal's response.

—Anticipate your response.

—End the conversation with grace.

5. Review the reasons we don't ask for forgiveness. Which of these are reasons you have used? Under each one you have used, describe the results of not forgiving.

— "If we don't talk about it, I'm sure the problem will just go away."

— "It's not all my fault."

— "I didn't mean to hurt him."

— "Surely he's over it by now."

— "Surely he's forgotten."

— "I'll just do it again."

— "I'm angry at him, and I won't forgive until he apologizes to me first."

— "I don't know how he'll respond."

— "If I ask for forgiveness, I'll have to change."

6. What will be your next step in taking action to ask for forgiveness?

CHAPTER 5

PRINCIPLE #3: LOVE YOUR CHILD UNCONDITIONALLY

*L*et me tell you the story of two fathers whose families attend the same church in Tennessee. Both had daughters in high school. One day several years ago, Joe's daughter, a 17-year-old junior, walked into the living room where he was reading the newspaper. She sat heavily on the sofa across the room without saying a word. Her eyes were red and swollen. After a few seconds, he noticed she was in the room with him, and he saw she had been crying. He put down his paper and asked, "What's wrong, honey?"

She looked down at the floor, "Mom told me I have to tell you myself." She began to sob.

Joe got up and crossed the room. He sat next to her on the sofa and put his arm around his dear daughter and told her, "Oh, it can't be that bad. Tell me what's going on."

"But it *is* that bad!" she shot back. "Daddy, I'm pregnant!"

Joe became rigid and tears welled up in his eyes, but not the tears of sorrow and compassion. His were tears of rage. After a long, tense moment, he stepped away from his daughter and growled, "How could you do this to me? You know how I've tried to raise you, and look what you've done!"

She was crying uncontrollably now, but he continued his tirade. "You listen to me. I don't want this baby, and I don't want you. Get your things together and leave right now! Don't ever set foot in this house again. Do you understand me?"

She nodded meekly.

As he stormed out the door, he added, "You have made me ashamed to be your father." His daughter left that afternoon.

Joe's friend Frank was the pastor of their church. Six months after Joe's daughter announced her pregnancy, Frank told the congregation that he wanted to speak on a personal subject for a minute in church that morning. He swallowed hard and began, "I want to tell you about something before you hear it from anywhere else. I asked my daughter if I could tell you, and she said yes. My 16-year-old daughter, Marianne, is pregnant, and as you know, she's not married. She told me the other day and her heart was broken. She said, 'Dad, I've messed up, and I'm so sorry. Will you please forgive me?' She expected me to get angry, but my heart was filled with love for my sweet daughter. I put my arms around her, and I told her, 'I love you so much. There's nothing in the world you could do to keep me from loving you.'

"She looked at me through her tears and asked, 'But Dad, what about your position in the church? What will people say . . . about you?'

"I told her clearly, 'Darling, I don't care if they fire me from the pastorate or if they ask me to resign. I'm going to stand by you, no matter what.' So I want you all to know today that my daughter is pregnant. We don't believe in abortion, so she will have the baby. Whatever assistance she needs, my wife and I will gladly provide for her. I don't approve of what she did, but she is my daughter and I love her."

> **Guess which daughter is walking with God today?**

Guess which daughter is walking with God today? That's a pretty easy one, isn't it? Joe's daughter is lonely, bitter, and has experienced several failed marriages. She feels far away from her father, who is still ashamed of her, and far away from God as well. Frank's daughter is a vibrant Christian who has a wonderful ministry to unwed mothers.

Love and bitterness are both incredibly powerful. One has the power to heal; the other has the power to kill. Parents of prodigals are challenged to respond like the father of the prodigal in Luke 15, with unconditional love. We don't have to approve of the prodigals' behavior, but we affirm that we love them no matter what they've done and continue to do.

WHY WE DON'T LOVE UNCONDITIONALLY

Many parents are terribly embarrassed by their prodigals. Sometimes after I talk about this subject in churches and conferences, parents come up to tell me I don't understand. They explain in whispers that their child is a homosexual . . . or in prison . . . or living with another woman . . . or whatever. Then they follow this revelation with the self-evident disclosure, "And I am so embarrassed."

Let me make this very clear: Just because your child is living in sin, you have no right to love him or her less. You don't need to approve of your prodigal's behavior, but you are commanded by God to love the person anyway. Unconditional love means we love our children for who they are, not what they have done.

As we noted in the first chapter, when we have one child living in sin and another walking with God, many of us portray one all bad and one all good. We can't see any of the positive things the sinning child is doing, and we overlook the faults of the "good child." Black-and-white comparisons make us less aware of the truth about both of them, and our love becomes more and more conditional as we deride one and elevate the other. Gossip and comparison drive the prodigal farther and farther away from God and from the family.

> **Some parents defend themselves by saying they don't want it to look as if they approve of sinful actions.**

Some parents defend themselves by saying they don't want it to look as if they approve of sinful actions. But everyone who knows them is well aware that they disapprove of their prodigal's sinful behavior. Don't use that excuse to keep you from loving your child.

Did God insist that you and I straighten up before He loved us?

Paul tells us clearly: "But God demonstrates His own love toward us, in that while we were still sinners, Christ died for us" (Rom 5:8). "While we were still sinners." That's when Christ made the supreme sacrifice and showed the depth of His great love toward us! Do you think Jesus' loving actions meant that He approved of our sins? Of course not, but Jesus didn't demand that we stop sinning before He loved us. If He had, we would be in terrible shape, wouldn't we?

Think of the Prodigal Son's father. That fine Jewish man, probably a leader in his community and his synagogue, had a son who was living with prostitutes and wasting money left and right. As if that weren't bad enough, then word came back that he had lost everything and was now feeding hogs! What could be more embarrassing? But that father didn't let anything—neither his embarrassment nor the whispers of his friends—cause him to love his son any less. The moment his son returned, he was eager to pour out his love. Any embarrassment was completely overwhelmed by love.

A second reason we may fail to love our prodigals is bitterness. We become angry with them for acting so foolishly, our anger gradually turns to resentment, and resentment festers into bitterness. The writer to the Hebrews recognized the threat that bitterness poses to relationships:

"Pursue peace with all men, and holiness, without which no one will see the Lord; looking diligently lest anyone fall short of the grace of God; lest any root of bitterness springing up trouble you, and by this many be defiled" (Heb 12:14-15).

When Debbie and I married, I had a small garden. As I weeded it the first year, many of the weeds broke off just above the ground. They looked like they were gone, but in a few days a new weed was growing strong from the roots. I learned (very quickly, I might add) that I had to dig out the roots of the weed to prevent it from growing back. In the same way, dealing with surface emotions and trying to look calm for our church friends doesn't solve the problem of bitterness. A root of bitterness troubles everyone it touches. It has to be yanked out to ensure it doesn't spread. We have to eradicate the whole root of bitterness if we are to live in love and peace.

> **Bitterness eats away at our hearts and consumes us. It creates feelings of self-righteousness.**

Bitterness prevents any closure or healing of pain. It leaves us desiring revenge instead of healing and compassion. We may not think of our angry behavior as revenge, but that's exactly what it is when we gossip about our prodigal, when we withdraw from her, when we find subtle ways of hurting him by giving a better gift to the "good child," or when we feel joy when the prodigal experiences hardships. We call it "justice" when he gets what we think he deserves, but "revenge" is a more accurate term.

And frankly, our bitterness probably affects us much more than it does our prodigals. It wastes our precious time on negative, destructive thoughts when we could be thinking of ways to honor God and help people. It eats away at our hearts and consumes us. It creates feelings of self-righteousness.

Frederick Buechner wrote about the effect bitterness has on us:

"Of the Seven Deadly Sins, anger is possibly the most fun. To lick your wounds, to smack your lips over grievances long past, to roll over your tongue the prospect of bitter confrontations still to come, to savor the last toothsome morsel both the pain you are given and the pain you are giving back— in many ways it is a feast fit for a king. The chief drawback is that what you are wolfing down is yourself. The skeleton at the feast is you."[3]

Bitterness saps our spiritual vitality. The Holy Spirit is grieved when we harbor resentment instead of forgiving and loving, and our joy in the Lord erodes day by day. We may still attend church services, sing the hymns, and even be in leadership, but gradually we begin to doubt God. We wonder, "How could God love me if He allows my son to do something like that?" Or, "Is God really sovereign? Is He really good?" If we don't root out the bitterness in our lives, we can pray for months and years with our prayers seemingly going unheard. We are initially hopeful, then disappointed, and eventually discouraged.

---

3 Frederick Buechner, *Wishful Thinking: A Theological ABC* (San Francisco: Harper and Row Publishers, 1973), p. 2.

Many Christians have great difficulty acknowledging their anger toward their prodigals because they've been taught that "good Christians don't get angry." So they smile through their bitterness and claim, "I'm not really angry, just disappointed." But this lack of honesty prevents them from opening their minds to God's truth and their hearts to His grace and power. They stay locked in a prison of bitterness: alone and hopeless.

A third reason we fail to love our prodigals is that we have developed a habit of living at arm's length from them. In the beginning, we tried everything we knew to do to help them change. When that didn't work, we felt resigned to a degree of coolness and distance in the relationship. We avoided talking about the real hurts and problems because they were just too painful. And besides, discussions about those things only brought more anger and discouragement. It was easier just to back off.

Distance begins as an emotional cushion, but quickly becomes a powerful barrier. Soon it becomes the norm for the relationship and we can hardly imagine what it would be like to relate any other way. We become convinced: "I'm right. He's wrong. No change." Love, however, doesn't use being right as an excuse to avoid reaching out to others. Jesus reached out to prostitutes and tax collectors. The loving father reached out to the Prodigal Son even though his son was terribly wrong. Love shines brightest when sin is darkest.

> **Love, however, doesn't use being right as an excuse to avoid reaching out to others.**

I L O V E Y O U I F . . .

The Bible describes three kinds of love: *eros* (sexual love), *phileo* (brotherly love), and *agape* (unconditional love). Our friendships are based on brotherly love. We are attracted to people because we have something in common with them: fishing, quilting, football, gardening, politics, or some other interest. As Christians, we are called to a higher form of love, *agape*, the way God loves us.

Brotherly love may be conditional: "I love you *if. . . ,*" or "I love you *when. . . .*" But *agape* love has no conditions: "I love you *in spite of. . . .*" Far too often, we love people only because they make us feel good or contribute to our welfare in some way. Many of us love our families based on some list of mental criteria and conditions. If our loved ones meet our requirements, we smile and compliment them. If they don't measure up, we scowl and walk away. Of course, parents of prodigals often can't find much to smile about. Their scowls have become permanent fixtures on their faces.

What are some of the criteria we expect to be met? Here are a few examples of messages that some parents communicate in their attitudes and expressions, if not in these exact words:

- I'll love you if you are nice to me.
- I love you when you make me look good in front of my friends.
- I love you when you come to church and walk with God.

- I'll love you if you will get a good job like your sister has.
- I'll love you if you take time to call me every Sunday afternoon.
- I'll love you if you'll pay me back what you owe me.
- I'll love you if you'll stop neglecting your children.
- I'll love you if stop acting like a fool and do what I think is right.

Jesus directs us to a higher definition of love. He tells us:

"But I say to you who hear: Love your enemies, do good to those who hate you, bless those who curse you, and pray for those who spitefully use you" (Luke 6:27-28).

This sounds like the testimony of many parents of prodigals, doesn't it? Some of our children hate us and curse us, and some spitefully use us. Even so, Jesus instructs us to take loving action toward them: do good to them, bless them, and pray for them. He continues:

"For if you love those who love you, what credit is that to you? For sinners also love those who love them. And if you do good to those who do good to you, what credit is that to you? Even sinners do the same. And if you lend to those from whom you hope to receive back, what credit is that to you? For sinners also lend to sinners to receive as much back. But love your enemies, do good, and lend, hoping for nothing in return; and your reward will be great, and you will be sons of the Highest. For He is kind to the unthankful and evil. Therefore be merciful, just as your Father also is merciful" (Luke 6:32-36).

Let me draw a few conclusions from this passage:

- Being kind to those who are kind to you is no big deal to God. Even the heathen do that.
- If we go beyond what is normal and extend genuine love to those who don't love us, we are acting more like God. He is thrilled when we attempt to be kind to unthankful and evil people!
- Real love is openhanded, "expecting nothing in return." Our love for others is genuine when we can't assume they will appreciate it, and even when we are *sure* they won't.
- If we choose to love those who don't love us, we will receive a reward someday. The reward *may* be the return of our loved ones, but that depends on them as well. We can only know that in this life or in the life to come, God will smile on us and reward us for our courage to love the unlovable.

> **Our love to others is genuine when we can't assume they will appreciate it, and even when we are *sure* they won't.**

YOU CAN'T GIVE WHAT YOU DON'T POSSESS

God doesn't expect us to draw water from an empty well. We can't give something that we don't possess, so God has gone to great lengths to give us the resources we need in order to offer unconditional love to others. I want to look at three passages of Scripture that encourage me. I trust God will use them to encourage you, too.

Accept others, just as you have been accepted.

In his letter to the Roman believers, Paul wrote, "Therefore receive one another, just as Christ also received us, to the glory of God" (Rom 15:7). Our ability to accept others, especially those whose behavior is unacceptable, is found in the fact that Christ has already accepted us. Paul had already written that we were helpless and hopeless enemies of God before we trusted Christ. That's pretty unacceptable, isn't it? Yet God reached out to us and graciously met us where we were. I think of all the examples of Jesus taking time to interact with prostitutes, tax collectors, children, rigid religious people, confused people, and anyone who wanted to know Him. Many of these people were unacceptable to others, but Jesus gladly accepted them without condemnation. He saw past the rough, sin-stained exteriors and looked at their hearts. He saw needs, and He met them.

Forgive others, just as you have been forgiven.

Paul also reminds us that our ability to forgive those who hurt us is based on our experience of God's forgiveness for our own sins. He wrote, "Let all bitterness, wrath, anger, clamor, and evil speaking be put away from you, with all malice. And be kind to one another, tenderhearted, forgiving one another, just as God in Christ also has forgiven you" (Eph 4:31-32).

If someone is unwilling or unable to forgive an offense, this passage suggests that the person is deficient in his or her personal experience of forgiveness. To put it another way, to the degree that we have experienced and are aware of God's forgiveness, we will be able and willing to forgive those who hurt us, including our prodigals.

Love others, just as you have been loved.

The apostle John identified himself in his gospel as "the disciple Jesus loved." Did that mean he was the only one Jesus loved? Of course not, but the love of Jesus was so convincing and overwhelming that it became the very basis of John's identity. "I'm the guy Jesus loves so much," he might have told people along the road as the disciples followed their Master. And we find in John's writings a gentleness and kindness that flowed from his personal experience of the love of Christ. He wrote, "In this is love, not that we loved God, but that He loved us and sent His Son to be the propitiation for our sins. Beloved, if God so loved us, we also ought to love one another" (I John 4:10-11).

Propitiation is an important word in our understanding of God. It means "to avert wrath." You and I, because of our sins, deserved the full wrath of God as His righteous judgment against our sinfulness. But Jesus' death on the cross was the sponge that absorbed all that wrath so you and I wouldn't have to experience it. Thanks to Jesus, in place of judgment, God showers us with love. Instead of the fires of hell, we receive His gracious presence. The punishment we so rightly deserved, Christ took in our place.

That is the measure of the love of God, so John can then apply that measure to our human relationships and say, "Beloved, if God so loved us, we also ought to love one another." Since the death of Christ averted God's righteous wrath so He could show us love, surely you and I can learn to show kindness to those who have not measured up to our petty standards.

> **Do these passages create a longing in your heart? Do you want to show this kind of unconditional love, forgiveness, and acceptance to your prodigal, but you simply don't know how?**

Do these passages create a longing in your heart? Do you want to show this kind of unconditional love, forgiveness, and acceptance to your prodigal, but you simply don't know how? We can't give them until we first let God work deeply and powerfully in our own hearts. Then, out of the abundance of our own experience, we can offer these treasures to others.

One time Jesus went to the Temple for the Feast of Tabernacles. Each day of the eight-day feast was more important than the day before. By the last day, the emotional and spiritual energy of the crowd of pilgrims had built to a crescendo. In the middle of the commotion, Jesus made an important announcement:

> "On the last day, that great day of the feast, Jesus stood and cried out, saying, 'If anyone thirsts, let him come to Me and drink. He who believes in Me, as the Scripture has said, out of his heart will flow rivers of living water.' But this He spoke concerning the Spirit, whom those who believe in Him would receive" (John 7:37-39).

We can't fake *agape* love. We can't produce it ourselves, but it is available to us in abundance if we recognize our thirst and go to Jesus. In our need, we drink deeply of His grace. We learn that He forgives us even when our hearts have been hard or when we have let Him down. We experience His kindness when we are hurting, and we discover the depth of His love when we realize how unlovable we really are. As the Holy Spirit works these truths into our hearts, we find a deep, full well of love, forgiveness, and acceptance for our prodigals—and for everyone else.

STEPS TO TAKE

I'm absolutely sure you want to love your prodigal unconditionally, or you wouldn't be reading this book. You may struggle with bitterness, and you may be embarrassed by your prodigal's behavior, but love covers a multitude of sins—yours and your prodigal's. Let me give you some specific steps to take to begin to show a deeper level of love.

1. Be honest about your lack of love.

First, be honest with God. If the Holy Spirit has let you know that your attitudes, words, and actions have been unkind toward your prodigal, agree with Him. Maybe your sin is that you have failed to love your prodigal with the unconditional love of Christ. All of us have failed that supreme test to some degree, but some of us have failed it miserably. Let God's Spirit shine His light on your heart and give you insight about the quality and depth of your love for your prodigal.

2. Experience God's love, forgiveness, and acceptance.

Don't rush out to act on the next few steps until you have spent plenty of time letting God's grace sink deep into your own heart. Maybe you should reread this chapter a time or two. It may be a good idea to pray through the passages we've addressed. Ask God to open your heart to comprehend His love more deeply than you've ever known it before. Focus on your own experience of agape love before you try to express it to your prodigal.

3. Take action.

In their excellent book, *The Blessing*, John Trent and Gary Smalley outline the ways the patriarchs gave blessings to their children. Abraham gave the blessing to Isaac (Genesis 25), Jacob schemed to take away Isaac's blessing from his brother Esau (Genesis 27), and Jacob then blessed his sons (Genesis 49). Trent and Smalley suggest that all parents can give a blessing to their children that will provide confidence, hope, and strength. I want to adapt their suggestions for parents of prodigals. We can give our sons and daughters a blessing by offering affirming words, meaningful touch, third-party compliments, meaningful gifts, and quality time.

Affirming words

Stop nagging. Stop condemning. Stop withholding kindness. Paul wrote, "Let no corrupt communication proceed out of your mouth, but what is good for necessary edification, that it may impart grace to the hearers" (Eph 4:29). Here's my translation of Paul's words: Shut up if you can't say something positive, and be sure to say things that encourage. (No wonder I've never been asked to write a translation of the Bible!)

> **You can't expect to speak words of grace if all your thoughts condemn a person. The battle is fought primarily in our thought-life. Fight hard, trust God, and win the battle.**

Our words come more from our heads than from our mouths. In other words, what we think about influences what we say. Analyze your thoughts to determine if they honor God and edify the person who hears them. If they meet that standard, keep on thinking them! If not, replace them with positive thoughts.

Many of us think we have no control over our minds, but that simply isn't true. We are stewards of our minds just as much as we are of our wallets and schedules. You can't expect to speak words of grace if all your thoughts condemn a person. The battle is fought primarily in our thought-life. Fight hard, trust God, and win the battle.

Look for things your prodigal does well. You may have to look hard to find something positive to say, and to be honest, you may have gotten out of practice after years of bitterness. But learn again how to find and speak affirming words. If you practice diligently and trust God for wisdom, they'll come.

An elderly man was on his deathbed. His wife had died years before, and he wanted to speak some final words to two of his nephews and a niece, all of whom were prodigals. Their mother (his sister) and their father had died years before. When the three adult children dutifully came to see him, he told them, "I love you so much. I'm really proud of you, and I know your mother would be very proud of you. You boys are both very successful in your businesses." He turned to his niece, who had taught in high school, and told her, "You are a wonderful teacher. Your students are so blessed to have you care for them and teach them. You have modeled fine character for them every day. I know they will remember you the rest of their lives."

After his words of genuine praise, the old man continued, "But there's one thing that breaks my heart. You aren't in church any more. You have all accomplished so much, but you are missing out on something that means a lot to me—a relationship with God. Before I die, I sure wish each of you would make a commitment to go back to church and walk with God."

The two nephews fidgeted, looked away, and mumbled, "We'll think about it." But the man's niece looked at him and said, "I promise you, next Sunday I'll go back to church and get my life right with God. I promise I'll walk with God the rest of my life."

Sure enough, that same week she was in church where she recommitted her life to Christ. Now, years later, she is strong in her faith and teaches Sunday school. She looks back on that day when her uncle affirmed her as a person, and in the context of his love asked her to commit herself to God. If he had used guilt, she would have backed away, but because he opened the door with kindness, she listened and responded.

Be sure you don't go overboard when you start using affirming words. If you say too much too soon, it will sound phony. It is better to say a word or two sincerely than to back up the dump truck with too many insincere compliments! And when you begin, expect nothing in return. Your prodigal may be caught off guard, and might even get angry because you waited so long to say things he longed to hear years ago. He may even have given up on hearing them, and will feel uncomfortable when you do express yourself. So speak simply and sparingly at first, and always with complete honesty.

Meaningful touch

Psychologists confirm what we know instinctively: physical touch is one of the most powerful ways to communicate love to someone. A kind hug or a pat on the back can mean more than you know to one who considers himself an outcast. Some families are "huggers," and some aren't. In the families that hug a lot, *not* hugging a prodigal communicates that he is an outcast, unwanted and unaccepted. So in your attempt to reconcile, you may need to ask for permission to hug him again. Don't despair if he refuses out of his deep hurt. Your attempt is the first step toward opening the door to meaningful interaction, including hugging again when the time is right.

In the case of families who never tended to hug much, touch is not an option. It is a necessity to show genuine affection to someone you love in order to fill in the holes left by a lifetime of neglect. If hugging seems to be too threatening for the person, try a pat on the hand or the back, or simply a handshake.

Third-party compliments

Have you ever noticed how children beam with delight and pride when their parents tell a friend about their accomplishments in their presence? My children do. Third-party compliments are powerful when wanting to assure someone you are sincere in your appreciation. Tell a friend, neighbor, or family member what you admire about your prodigal. If he's standing there, fine; if not, maybe he will hear about it later. Either way, you are sowing seeds of kindness and confidence. Who knows when and where they will spring up and bloom?

Meaningful gifts

Some of us have used gifts as attempts to manipulate wayward family members. We have given in order to get something, or we have withheld gifts to make a point or to punish them. Some of us have given our prodigals 348 audiotapes on topics such as "How to Turn Your Life

Around," "Stop Being Foolish," or "Repent, You Prodigal!" If you're guilty of such "giving," stop. Instead, think about what the person values and give a present that says, "I understand what's important to you, and I love you." Consider giving a present at a time that doesn't require one. The gift doesn't have to be expensive at all, just something thoughtful.

Quality time

Some parents manage to spend lots of time in the proximity of their prodigals—perhaps taking care of their kids or helping out in some other indirect way. Other parents have been so angry so long that they have lost touch with their prodigal sons and daughters. If you already spend time helping them, think about how you might use that time to interact more personally. For example, you might tell your prodigal some good news about a friend of his or hers (being very careful to avoid gossip). If your relationship is distant and strained, begin by writing letters. Later try some phone calls, and as the comfort level rises for both of you, consider face-to-face visits. Make the first personal visit very brief and positive. As your relationship is strengthened, you can begin to spend more time together.

4. Take the risk of loving.

The kind of love Jesus speaks of in Luke 6 is risky. He instructs us to give sacrificially, expecting nothing in return. If we harbor hopes that our prodigals will change magically and make us happy, we will probably be very disappointed. Genuine love always involves risk: the risk that we won't be appreciated, the risk that we will receive anger in return for kindness, or the risk that as we move toward our prodigals, they will move farther away.

We also take the risk that others in the community (and even in the church) will criticize us if we display unconditional love toward a prodigal. Their scorn toward the prodigal quickly spreads to anyone who supports him or her. We need to remember that Jesus took a lot of flak from the Pharisees for showing kindness to sinners. If you show love to your prodigal, you may catch flak from the "Pharisees" in your church, too. But if you recall, that was the very reason Jesus told the parable of the Prodigal Son. He wanted to show the rigid, self-righteous religious contingent that God's heart was big enough to forgive even sinners.

> If you show love to your prodigal, you may catch flak from the "Pharisees" in your church, too. But if you recall, that was the very reason Jesus told the parable of the Prodigal Son. He wanted to show the rigid, self-righteous religious contingent that God's heart was big enough to forgive even sinners.

But the risk of loving is always a risk worth taking. Jesus took that risk with every person on the planet. Some have embraced His offer of love, but many more have rejected Him. Some keep Him at arm's length, and others are confused by His grace. Yet no matter how we respond, He keeps reaching out again and again to show His love. He is the example we should follow in our relationships with those to whom we desperately want to communicate love and peace.

WATCH FOR SIBLING JEALOUSY

The most bitter person in some families is a sibling of the prodigal. We all want attention, but in those families most of the attention goes to the one who is ruining his own life and hurting others. The faithful sibling often thinks, "I'm good to my parents, I go to church, and I pay my bills. I haven't been arrested, so nobody had to sit through my trial. I'm a responsible person, but my brother is a bum! Yet look at all they do for him!"

The "good kid" longs for his parents to spend as much time thinking about him, talking about him, and praying for him as they do for his "no-good" sibling. He resents that sibling for soaking up so much of the focused attention he wants to receive.

In addition, the wayward sibling may be squandering the "good kid's" inheritance. The prodigal may have stolen money from his parents, or they may have shelled out tens of thousands of dollars in bail money. They may have "loaned" him great amounts of cash, realizing they aren't likely to get back a dime of it. The "good kid" knows much of that wealth probably would have been his one day.

The responsible child also feels he isn't being rewarded for doing the right thing. He feels he deserves his parents' blessings for being responsible, and he certainly doesn't think he should be overlooked. The prodigal is being rewarded with time and money while he, the responsible one, feels left out in the cold.

And if the "good kid" is jealous when his parents bail out his prodigal sibling, he may become genuinely furious when the prodigal comes home and the parents forgive him! In Jesus' parable, the Prodigal Son's brother was intensely jealous when he heard the celebration of his brother's return, and he griped to his father. It wasn't fair! That's the same sentiment many siblings of prodigals feel.

Watch for potential problems with sibling jealousy, and do all you can to speak the truth. You might need to apologize for times you have shown preference to your prodigal over your responsible children. Show plenty of love to the ones who have been faithful. Don't give them a reason to be jealous.

Also be sure to write a clear will that outlines your intentions for how you want your estate to be divided. Don't assume your children will figure things out on their own and get along just fine. If one of them has been a prodigal, they probably won't.

LOVE OTHER PARENTS OF PRODIGALS

Perhaps the only people in your church who know what you are going through are other parents of prodigals. They have experienced the same pains and challenges, so we need to be their most committed and enthusiastic supporters!

I recently talked to a woman whose son is an alcoholic and pathological liar. Years ago, he married a woman whose mother was a good friend of his mom's. These two women had been friends since childhood, and they took to being in-laws with great enthusiasm. To no one's surprise, the marriage failed. The son lost all the money he made and ruined his reputation—again. The daughter had multiple affairs, just like she had done before they married. Yet instead of comforting one another, the two mothers blamed each other's child—and each other—for the failed relationship. It has been 15 years since the divorce. They still live in the same small town and go to the same church, yet they still haven't spoken to each other in all that time.

Every parent of a prodigal can come up with plenty of reasons to feel hurt and angry at their son or daughter. But we need to move beyond those things and focus on sources of healing, love, and grace—first for ourselves, and then for our children who are desperate for our unconditional acceptance.

Sometimes parents think loving their children unconditionally means they must continually remove the pain and fix the problems in the lives of their prodigals, but that's not true. We also show love—tough love—by allowing sin to run its course. We'll examine that demonstration of love in the next chapter.

1. Are any of the three reasons cited in this chapter for not loving prodigals true for you? Under the one(s) you have used, describe your attitude and actions, and how this has affected you and your relationship with your prodigal.

— Embarrassment

— Bitterness

— Habit

2.   How have you seen bitterness destroy lives and rela-
     tionships?

3.   How have you seen love rebuild relationships?

4.   In your own words, describe the differences between
     agape (unconditional love) and phileo (brotherly love).

5. Review the section in this chapter under the heading, "You Can't Give What You Don't Possess." In what ways do you need to experience more of God's love, forgiveness, and acceptance?

What difference will your experience of God's love make in how you relate to your prodigal?

6. Write out a plan for taking action by communicating:

— Affirming words

— Meaningful touch

— Third-party compliments

— Meaningful gifts

— Quality time

7. What risks will you be taking if you love your prodigal unconditionally?

8. Is sibling jealousy a problem in your family? What is the "good kid" jealous about? What changes do you need to make, if any, to help resolve this problem?

Principle #4: Allow Sin to Run Its Course

A mother in her 70's has a 50-year-old son and two younger daughters. The son, Rick, is very bright—except when it comes to work, women, money, and booze. Rick's father died when he was just a boy, and the family struggled financially. His mother worked very hard to provide a decent life for her three children, but that was in the days before the movement for equal pay for women. Though she rose to a significant position as loan officer at a bank, her salary remained far lower than the men she worked with.

As the children grew up, it was evident that Rick was a gifted young man, but he was also filled with anger and insecurity. He began to drink when he was in high school, and his social drinking soon was out of control. He was arrested for driving while intoxicated, but he told his mother he'd only had "a couple of beers." She believed him. She blamed the policeman for being so harsh for "such a small offense," and she paid his fine.

After graduating from college, and after several more arrests and fines which his mother paid, Rick got a job and got married. Neither his job nor his marriage proved exciting enough for him, so he bailed out of both. His mother believed the problem was Rick's employer and his wife because that's what Rick told her.

Rick had great ideas to start new businesses, but none of his friends would become partners with him. Finally, he became desperate. He asked his mother for a loan. He promised to repay her within a year . . . eighteen months at the most. But after only seven months the business folded, and neither Rick nor his mother mentioned the "loan" for a long time.

Rick took jobs with new companies in the budding fields of technology, but he never liked working for somebody else. After a year or so, he found someone who would loan him some money for another new venture. This venture capitalist, though, was unwilling to put up all the money. Rick still needed about $15,000 more, so he called his mother and excitedly told her about this new deal. He explained that he'd be able to pay her back the $15,000 plus the money he'd lost on the first business deal. She was skeptical, and this time she consulted her attorney. Her lawyer suggested a binding legal agreement, but she didn't want to upset her son with demanding language, so she had him sign a watered-down version before she loaned him the money. Within a few months his new venture went bankrupt and all his mother had was a worthless piece of paper with his good intentions written on it.

Rick's drinking problem grew worse along with his financial problems. He was arrested again for driving while intoxicated, and this time was taken to jail. He called his mother and told her, "If I don't post bail, they say they'll keep me for a week!"

His mother simply couldn't let that happen, so she drove down to the police station and bailed him out. Outside the jail, she demanded, "Son, I'm sick of this! You'd better never let this happen again!"

> **Outside the jail, she demanded, "Son, I'm sick of this! You'd better never let this happen again!"**

Rick meekly replied, "You're right, Mom. This is the last time." She drove away in furious silence.

As a result of his latest arrest, Rick's license was revoked. He had another job, but no way to get there. His solution? He called his mother and got her to take him to work every day for a few weeks. She was angry at being used like this, but she knew that he needed to work to pay her back. When he couldn't stand the shame of being dropped off and picked up by his mother (like a preschool kid), Rick started driving again, well before the date set by the judge.

Rick's love life wasn't any better than his business life. He was married two more times, and each time got a divorce within a year or so. His ex-wives took furniture his mother had given him, pieces she had treasured and hoped he would value, too. But for each marriage disaster, he had plenty of excuses. His wives were too bossy; his mothers-in-law were too demanding and "bad-mouthed" him behind his back; or his wives expected to live the high life that he simply couldn't provide for them. His mother took his side each time and defended him to family friends, some of whom knew both Rick and his ex-wives very well.

One day two IRS agents visited Rick at work and ordered him to appear before a judge three days later. It turned out that he hadn't responded to their letters and demands over the last two years. He owed $22,000 in back taxes, penalties, and interest, and he was being arrested.

Rick called his mother and told her that he was in big trouble now. He might have to go to jail for three years if he couldn't come up with the money. His mother exploded, "Do you expect me to just give you $22,000? After all the money I've given you, you haven't paid back a dime!"

Rick protested, "That's not true, Mom. I paid you back $1000 last year when. . . ."

"A thousand dollars!" she interrupted. "You owe me almost a hundred thousand dollars, and you think paying me back $1000 is really something?"

> She asked her mother, "And what will it be next time? How much will he ask you for then? Mom, you need to put a stop to it now."

"Mom, this time I really mean it. If you'll loan me the $22,000, I'll pay you back within a year. I swear, Mom," he pleaded. "I swear. Please, Mom. I don't want to go to prison."

She thought about her dear son in prison for three years, and she couldn't bear the thought. She called her two daughters to get their opinions. Sarah was sympathetic: "Mom, I saw the movie *Shawshank Redemption*. We just can't let Rick go to prison! Horrible things happen there."

Suzanne, however, was more perceptive. She asked her mother, "And what will it be next time? How much will he ask you for then? Mom, you need to put a stop to it now."

Her mother was shocked by Suzanne's calloused attitude. She protested, "So you think it's a good idea for him to spend years in prison? After he gets out, he'll be a convicted felon. What kind of job can he get then? How will he pay me back if he can't get a job? Did you think of that?"

Suzanne stood firm. "If you keep bailing him out, he'll never learn his lesson. He'll just keep coming back for more. Look at his life since he graduated from college. It's been almost 30 years of non-stop trouble, and you have bailed him out every single time. He has made promises each time, and you've believed his lies. There's no end to it unless you stop bailing him out." Suzanne didn't mention that her mother hadn't offered to help her financially when she had needed some help years before.

Rick's mom spent a long, sleepless night thinking about the massive amount of money she'd "loaned" him, the string of broken promises, Suzanne's hard heart, and Rick's desperate situation. At nine the next morning, she called Rick and told him she would have to get a second mortgage on her house because all her savings were gone, but she would have a check for him by early the next morning. Rick expressed his deep gratitude, and he promised again and again that he'd pay her back every cent.

It's been nine years since that incident. Rick is still drinking and driving. He has gotten married and divorced again. He has paid back his mother a total of $1500 out of the almost $200,000 he now owes her, including the interest that is accruing. After all the threats and promises, anger and guilt, nothing has changed. Nothing at all.

TWO INGREDIENTS

Good relationships, either among family or friends, require a blend of two vital ingredients: closeness and independence. We must learn to love the other person, but without controlling him or her. Some call this "open-handed love" or "non-possessive warmth." We care for someone, but we let the other person make his own decisions.

If this delicate blend gets out of balance, we gravitate toward one of two extremes: isolation or enmeshment. In some cases, fear or anger drives us away from others. It is easier to be alone than to risk closeness. In other situations, that same fear and anger creates insecurity in the relationship, so we try to control the other person any way we can. We convince ourselves that our nagging and our demands are for that person's good. We spend much of our time fixing the person's problems and

> We convince ourselves that our nagging and our demands are for that person's good. We spend much of our time fixing the person's problems and anticipating his needs. We become consumed with his problems and needs.

anticipating his needs. We become consumed with his problems and needs. And goodness knows, prodigals certainly have lots of needs.

We come to believe that our sense of worth—our value as parents—is determined by how much we help our prodigals. When we fix them, we feel strong. If we fail, we feel worthless and guilty. So our motto becomes:

If my prodigal has a need, I'll meet it.
If he has a little need, I'll make it into a big need.
   Then I'll meet it.
If he doesn't have a need, I'll find one!

REASONS WE FIX THEM

Prodigals, especially the embarrassing and defiant ones, mess up their lives in incredible ways. They have financial calamities, trouble with the law, drinking and drug difficulties, and children who are neglected or out of control. They marry people we can't stand, and they make decisions that are foolish at best. We see all this very clearly, and we feel compelled to jump in to make it right.

Why are many parents of prodigals wired to fix their children's problems? Here are some reasons.

Their failure makes us look bad.

We are ashamed when others learn a child of ours has been arrested again, is on drugs, has lost yet another job, or has children who are running wild. We see our children as a reflection of us. If they look good, we look good. If they look bad. . . .

153

Every week in Sunday school, we hear updates on other people's children: Ralph's son is now dean of men at the University ("the youngest man ever to hold that position," Ralph beams) and Jenny's daughter has led 769,976 people to Christ as a missionary in Lower Slobovia. We're glad for Ralph and Jenny—but not *that* glad. We yearn to say something positive about our children, at least something better than, "Yes, we're really excited. Johnny's sentence was reduced from ten years to five. Isn't God wonderful?"

We hope they'll love us for helping them.

Let's face it: we all need love. We desperately want the members of our family to show us love and appreciation. So when they get in trouble, we think, "If I help him this once, surely he'll appreciate it. Surely he'll thank me. Surely he'll feel closer to me."

We perceive our help as a type of bargaining. We give something, hoping for something in return. We give money or time or whatever, and we hope our prodigals will love us for it. I've talked to many parents who have a look of complete confusion on their faces when they tell me about all the ways they've helped their prodigals and then conclude, "But no matter what I do, she doesn't appreciate it. In fact, we seem farther apart now than when I started helping her."

> **"But no matter what I do, she doesn't appreciate it. In fact, we seem farther apart now than when I started helping her."**

They demand our help.

Prodigals become masters of manipulation. They whine that if we love them we will call them in sick, or give them money, or take care of their kids while they're gone, or whatever. They often have a "victim mentality," and they demand that other people fix their problems. "It's not my fault!" they protest, and they heap loads of guilt on their parents for saying or doing anything they don't feel is completely loving and nurturing. These prodigals, however, fail to look in the mirror and see that they are now adults who are responsible for their own decisions.

We are motivated by tremendous guilt.

Parents mess up sometimes. No doubt about it. We fail our children in numerous ways, and we feel awful about it. When our prodigals demand that we fix their problems, it triggers our compulsion to compensate for our shortcomings by doing whatever it takes to make them happy.

We become like puppets on a string: They pull; we dance. Guilt clouds our sense of self-esteem and security. It drives us to make decisions we would never make otherwise. People who are normally good money managers give thousands of dollars to an irresponsible child because they feel so terrible about the negative influence they had on him. Maybe the parents can readily identify that influence, such as their own alcoholism, frequent rage between them, or a divorce. But in many cases, they can't pinpoint a clear cause for the problem. They simply surmise, "Since my child is having all these problems, it must be my fault."

Fixing Is a Hindrance

Every adult, including your prodigal, is responsible for his or her own behavior. Every adult is accountable to God and to family and friends for his decisions. When parents jump in to fix a prodigal's problems, they block God's redemptive work in that person's life. They hinder God from doing what He wants to do to bring change and redemption in that prodigal's heart.

Think back once more to the Prodigal Son after the "mighty famine" hit and he took a job slopping hogs. It was as he longed to eat the pods the pigs were eating, facing abject desperation, that "he came to himself." That's when his pride was thoroughly broken, and he was at last ready for complete repentance and a return home.

What do you think would have been the outcome if his father had sent him sandwiches and soup every day? What if his dad had wired him some cash "just this once" to help him get through that hard time? But his father allowed him to continue to try to make it on his own, even with all his bad decisions, until he finally saw his deep needs and gained spiritual perspective.

> **What if his dad had wired him some cash "just this once" to help him get through that hard time?**

This is a crucial lesson for the parents of prodigals. We simply must follow the example of the father in Jesus' parable and let our beloved children experience the consequences of their decisions. If we step in and fix them, we short-circuit God's redemptive work. We find ourselves opposing God instead of working in tandem with Him.

As loving parents, we hate to see our children suffer. We want them to be whole, happy, and healthy, and we may be blinded by our deep desire, coupled with guilt. We keep fixing them over and over again, and we shield them from the stark realities of life. We prevent them from being angry with us and accusing us of not caring, but by removing the consequences of their actions, we also prevent them from growing.

Threats, and Other Lies

"This is the last time I'm going to bail you out! Do you understand me? The last time!" How many times have parents spoken like this to their prodigals? Almost every parent of a prodigal has gotten into a pattern of using threats, but they seldom if ever follow through with the consequences of the threat.

The prodigal, too, threatens to never speak to his parents again if they don't come through for him. He may even threaten to kill himself if they don't help him. In each predicament, he always insists, "This is the last time." But then, so do parents. We promise we are stepping in for the last time, just as he promises he'll never ask us again. But as we are both well aware, these are lies.

We train each other to disregard our words, because actions are what really matter. One prodigal told me, "When I'm in trouble, my mother yells at me and fusses at me, but in the end, she always comes through." Underneath all the threats and promises, both parent and prodigal know that no amount of yelling, blaming, arguing, sulking, or crying will change things. Too many parents are simply unwilling to make the hard decision to quit bailing out their wayward kids.

In the place of truth, parents offer excuses for why their children keep ruining their lives. They say:

- "She can't help it. She's always been that way."
- "It's not his fault he got fired. His boss is a real jerk— just like the last one."
- "Oh, divorce isn't all that bad. The grandkids will probably be better off anyway."
- "I'm sure it won't happen again. Look at all the trouble it caused. Surely he'll learn from this mistake."

These, too, are forms of lies. Such excuses attempt to minimize the damage and excuse the foolish person from taking responsibility for poor, destructive decisions. Facing reality is incredibly difficult for our prodigals, but it is just as difficult for the parents. Yet we are lying to ourselves if we think we are genuinely helping them.

Dr. James Dobson wrote a best-selling book entitled *Love Must Be Tough*, in which he addresses this very point. Fixing prodigals doesn't help them at all. In the long run, it hurts them. Threats sound tough. They allow us to bluster and sound authoritative, but if we don't follow through with what we say we're going to do, our words are hollow.

In fact, we lose ground because our children learn that our words cannot be trusted.

HOW DOES FIXING HURT THE PRODIGAL?

Attempting to fix all our children's problems can be more devastating for them than we realize. It may bring temporary relief, but in the long run it prevents them from learning valuable lessons that can change their lives. Consider the following potential results when parents get too involved too often.

> **Facing reality is incredibly difficult for our prodigals, but it is just as difficult for the parents. Yet we are lying to ourselves if we think we are genuinely helping them.**

Creating false expectations

I've talked to men and women as old as 60 who tell me, "It doesn't matter how much I mess up. My parents will always find a way to fix things." These supposedly adult children have the psychological development of preschoolers. They have learned to be helpless because they know someone else will come along and make everything right for them. All they need to do is whine loud enough long enough, and the Lone Fixer will ride in and solve their problems. They have developed false—and dangerous—expectations.

Preventing justice

Prodigals whose problems are solved by their parents have a warped view of justice. They don't realize that people reap what they sow. Their parents have bypassed that important principle in their lives. Whenever they have a problem, they automatically seek an easy bailout. But ironically, when other people face difficulties, these same prodigals are often quick to condemn them for their foolishness.

Teaching them to be irresponsible

Pampered prodigals don't learn the hard lessons of responsibility. They become convinced that it's too much trouble to do what's right, and besides, it's not much fun anyway. They live for the pleasure of the moment and never learn to value time, money, people, or commitments. Becoming responsible requires wisdom and endurance. If parents bail out their children every time they have problems, they take them out of God's school of higher education and prevent them from learning crucial lessons. Rescuing prodigals reinforces their belief that they don't have to follow through with the decisions and commitments they've made.

Preventing brokenness

God "loves a contrite heart." Many of the psalms and other passages of Scripture tell us that God delights in people who realize they are humble and needy. Jesus said, "Blessed are the poor in spirit, for theirs is the kingdom of heaven" (Matt 5:3). Those who have been bailed out time and time again develop calluses over their hearts. Each instance adds another layer that makes it even more difficult for the prodigal to soften his heart. But nothing is too difficult for God. He wants your prodigal to "come home" even more than you do, and I'm convinced that many of the difficulties our prodigals face are orchestrated by God. We interfere with His work when we keep stepping in and preempting those messages.

Perpetuating manipulation

Lies and manipulation become a cycle between parents and prodigals as parents threaten but bail their kids out anyway, and in return the prodigals promise to change but don't follow through. It is like a dance that never ends, an ugly dance of controlling behavior, guilt, and ruined hopes.

By now you may be thinking, "But what about unconditional love? I just read the chapter on unconditional love, but now you are telling me to stop helping my child. If I do that, she'll believe I don't love her. I'm confused."

> **Unconditional love is much more than simply making someone happy for a while. It is doing whatever it takes for that person's ultimate well-being.**

Unconditional love is much more than simply making someone happy for a while. It is doing whatever it takes for that person's ultimate well-being. Unconditional love is usually wonderfully nurturing and affirming, but sometimes it must cut like a surgeon's scalpel in order to remove the tumor of sin. Sometimes a doctor must cause a little pain to affect long-term healing. In the same way, love dictates that we

161

speak the truth about irresponsible behavior and then require real change. Anything less is not love; it is only sentimentality, which is a poor substitute for the real thing.

The Courage to Stop Fixing

It may tell you more about me than I want you to know, but I love *The Andy Griffith Show*. Andy was a paragon of virtue, and Barney Fife was, well, Barney. In one episode, Andy's son Opie had a conniving friend, Arnold, who told him, "I know a way you can get anything you want from your dad."

"How can I do that?" Opie asks him.

"If you ask him and if he says 'no,' just hold your breath 'til you turn blue. He'll panic and give you anything then!"

"Wow!" exclaimed Opie. "I gotta try that!"

Opie went to the Sheriff's Office to see his father, and he asked him, "Pa, I want you to triple my allowance."

"Well," Andy began slowly, "I don't know about that, Opie. Naw, I just can't do that, son."

Opie insisted, "But I really want it, Pa!"

Andy was not going to give in. "No, Opie. I said you can't have it."

Opie took a deep breath and held it. Andy watched as Opie's face turned red. (It never did turn blue like Arnold said it would.) Finally, Opie couldn't hold it any longer, and he gasped for a breath. He looked confused, and Andy asked him, "Opie, what in the world are you doing?

Opie answered, "Holding my breath 'til you give me what I want."

"At least it's good for your lungs," Andy told him as he walked off.

Opie told Arnold that his trick didn't work, but Arnold was determined to do whatever he wanted, no matter what. Barney repeatedly told him to not ride his bike in the street, but Arnold ignored him. Finally, Barney told him to stay out of the street "or I'll impound your bike, young man. I sure will!" The boy didn't believe Barney's threat, and moments later he almost ran over Sheriff Taylor! Barney, ever the watchful deputy, saw the whole scene and made good on his promise. He grabbed Arnold and impounded his bike.

In the Sheriff's Office, Andy told the boy to bring his father in for a talk. Soon the father swaggered into the station and demanded, "Sheriff, you can give me the bike now."

Andy replied in his wise way, "It's not quite that simple. Your son needs to stay off the street, or I'm going to keep that bike until he learns his lesson. If he rides in the street one more time, I'll have to put you in jail."

> You can't expect to speak words of grace if all your thoughts condemn a person. The battle is fought primarily in our thought-life. Fight hard, trust God, and win the battle.

The boy pounded the sheriff's desk angrily and yelled at Andy, "You can put my daddy in jail, just give me my bike!"

The boy's father was surprised to see the extent of his son's selfishness. He turned to Andy and told him solemnly, "That's OK, Sheriff. Give me the bike. I'm going to sell it."

Hearing his father's words, the son pitched a fit. Andy watched the tirade, then told the father, "Sir, in case you're wondering, there's an old-fashioned woodshed out back." His father immediately led Arnold out back to have the board of education applied to the seat of learning.

Like the father in this episode of *The Andy Griffith Show,* some of us need to step back, take a good look at our prodigal's attitude and actions, and change our behavior. Righting wrongs requires courage. We have lived a lie long enough and something different must be done. No matter what it takes, we must become partners with God instead of roadblocks to His work.

The courage to stop fixing our prodigals requires three things: perspective, a plan, and support.

Perspective

A father told me his son lost his job again. He had always had problems holding a good job, and always blamed his boss, the company, vindictive coworkers, or something else for his failures. His father had believed him every time and had made calls to his friends to try to find his son a new job. Time after time, his friends pointed out, "His résumé and references aren't all that good." But the dad pleaded and promised, "This time will be different." His friends would reluctantly hire the young man, but after a few months the same patterns would emerge, and he would again be fired.

This loving father finally told his son, "I want you to look at what has happened in the last five places you've worked." His son started to defend himself, but the dad continued, "Son, both of us have to face the facts. You have lost these jobs because you have acted irresponsibly." Again, the son tried to jump to his own defense, but again the father silenced him. "And son, this has got to stop. First, I want you to know I'm not going to ask any of my friends for a job for you. That's final. You are going to have to find one on your own. I'm not going to support you while you are looking for a job. And I'm not going to lie to my friends about your problem. I won't say anything unless they want to know, but if they ask, I'm going to tell them you are learning some valuable lessons about responding to authority. I will be glad to advise you, but I'm not going to get involved directly any more. What I have done up to now hasn't helped, as much as I wanted it to. In fact, I really think all my efforts have hurt you by keeping you from being realistic about your behavior."

During this carefully planned statement, the son fumed. At his first opportunity he exploded in a tirade of accusations. "If Mother were here, she wouldn't let you get away with treating me like this! She loved me!" Then he growled, "I wish you had died instead of her!"

The father remained calm. "Sometimes I wish the same thing, Son. But I'm here and she's not. And actually, I've thought a lot about what your mother would want, and I'm convinced she would agree that if I really love you, I'll insist on more responsibility from you."

This father did a magnificent job of confronting reality and speaking with clarity and grace. He didn't yell. He didn't curse. He simply spoke the truth and explained what he was willing to do—and not do. All that was left

> When we see that threats and broken promises aren't working, change is absolutely mandatory. If we continue to believe lies and fix problems, we perpetuate irresponsibility.

was to follow through with what he had said.

When we see that threats and broken promises aren't working, change is absolutely mandatory. If we continue to believe lies and fix problems, we perpetuate irresponsibility. We need a new perspective that combines truth with a passionate hope that God will work to create a new life for our prodigals and for us.

Our new perspective also lets us see that we can't control our prodigals' behavior. We can speak truth and we can pray, but we need to let our prodigals make their own decisions. We muster the courage to open our hands and let go if they decide to turn their backs on us. We can only control our choices, not theirs. They are free to come or go, to act responsibly or irresponsibly. It is the best opportunity for allowing them to reach a point of repentance.

A Plan

Any time we chart a new course in any area of our lives, we need a plan. If you want to take up quilting, you learn from others, design your pattern, and find the fabric you'll need for the job. If you want to learn to fly fish, you watch people who have perfected the art of dropping a dry fly at the head of a pool so it can drift past a submerged rock where a trout is likely to be waiting for his next bite. We need a plan when we travel, plant a garden, bake a cake, or install software on our computers. And we need a plan when we want to make changes in the crucial relationships with our prodigals.

I suggest you write out your plan carefully, with the input of someone who has successfully dealt with the same problem. (Keep in mind that success isn't determined by the prodigal's response, but by the parents acting in a responsible way to avoid fixing the prodigal's problems any longer.) Your plan needs to focus on addressing the patterns you have seen in your prodigal and in yourself. They will be painfully obvious, so don't be shy about writing them clearly and boldly. Stay focused on the big things: irresponsible behavior, promises and threats, and meaningless gestures. Also list the excuses the two of you have used that prevented you from seeing the truth before.

In your plan, take responsibility for your own behavior. If you have believed lies, determine to quit. If you have been blocking God's work by fixing problems, admit as much.

A friend of mine who had been rescuing his sister for years began his talk with her by saying, "I want to apologize for the way I've treated you." She looked surprised. He continued, "I have bailed you out again and again. I hoped it would make you love me more, and I hoped it would make me feel good about myself. That was selfish of me, and sinful. Please forgive me." He then explained that he would no longer fix her problems.

Your plan needs to include a "next time" clause. Make it clear what you will do the next time your prodigal needs help. Some of us are so well-trained that we jump to help before we are even asked. Learn to say that word that all fixers must learn: "No." (It's not a long word, but it's powerful.)

> **Shortly after you tell your prodigal you aren't going to fix him any longer, you can be sure he will test you.**

Shortly after you tell your prodigal you aren't going to fix him any longer, you can be sure he will test you. Sooner or later, he'll have a crisis (it's always a crisis, isn't it?), and he will expect you to come to his rescue. Take a deep breath and say, "I'm sorry you're in trouble again, but like I told you, I'm not going to solve your problems any longer. I love you, and I want the very best for you. The best is for you in this case is to experience the consequences of your choices."

Your plan should also anticipate your child's reaction and prepare you for it. Be strong. Don't cave in to accusations. No matter how guilty you feel, don't give in and rescue the person again. Stay in control. If you anticipate these reactions, you won't be caught offguard.

Planning is a vital necessity in changing your relationship with your prodigal. Even if you are good at winging every other area of your life, this one is different. This relationship cuts to the core of who you are. It threatens you like nothing else in your life, so be prepared. Plan well.

Support

You've read the warnings on some toys, "Use only under adult supervision." The same is true for changing how we relate to prodigals. We benefit greatly from the insight, encouragement, and support of a trusted friend, pastor, or counselor. Most of us have flown solo for so long that we've been blinded to reality. We have called lies "truth," and we have excused sin. Now that we realize we need to change, we can be overwhelmed by the complexity and the confusion of the relationship. We aren't sure how much slack to give, if any, to our whining prodigals, and it's easy to go back to the old ways and rescue them "just one more time."

But choose your counselors wisely. Some people have simplistic solutions, like: "Just love him. Everything will turn out all right." Others like to avoid conflict in their own lives, so they advise you to do the same. A few will recommend drastic solutions, such as, "Kick him out and never let him see the door again! He deserves it!" And some spiritualize the relationship: "If you pray— really pray—I'm sure God will change your son's heart."

Perhaps you've heard such advice before. Each suggestion has a smattering of insight that makes it deceiving. Find someone who understands the difficult issues of responsibility and love, and draw wisdom and strength from that person as you go through this process of planning, communicating, and staying strong in your convictions.

The person who gives you perspective and encouragement may also clarify how you and your

> **Many of the heartaches parents of prodigals endure are not just with the prodigal. Others are caused by confusion and disagreement with a spouse or other children over the proper course of action.**

spouse have differed over how to handle your prodigal. In most families, the mother and father have very different solutions to the problem. One is passive, the other aggressive. One wants to avoid conflict, the other demands compliance. Many of the heartaches parents of prodigals endure are not just with the prodigal. Others are caused by confusion and disagreement with a spouse or other children over the proper course of action. Most couples try to talk about their disagreements in the early stages of the prodigal's difficulties, but frequently settle into patterns of quiet anguish or volcanic explosions that generate ongoing pain. Your pastor, counselor, or friend will notice how the strain of parenting a prodigal has affected your marriage, and you can seek healing in this relationship, too.

YOU CAN EXPECT . . .

We've already touched on this topic, but I now want to address it directly. When you stop fixing your prodigal's problems, you can expect him to fight you in every way he can. His goal is to get you to back down, to go back to the old way of rescuing him. He will do whatever it takes to make that happen.

You're already very familiar with his tactics, whether self-pity to melt your heart or vicious name-calling to coerce you into action. He may have accused you of not loving him "as much as you love" his brothers or sisters, who by the way, get far less of your time and attention than he does. He may even threaten to hurt himself if you don't come through this time. If he has made you feel guilty in the past, he'll try to make you feel guilty again. If he has intimidated you in the past, he'll do that again. Count on it. Be ready for it.

If you stay strong for a few days or a few weeks, don't think it is over. Like a prizefighter who holds back and waits for just the right opportunity, your prodigal may strike the moment you drop your guard. Many parents weather the initial onslaught and remain strong for a while, but are eventually caught unprepared and wilt under the pressure.

If you feel that you are going to cave in, buy some time. Say, "I need to think about this for a day or two. I'll get back to you." Then call your friend, counselor, or pastor to get the encouragement you need to stay strong. Whatever it takes, don't go back to the same destructive pattern that has been a dead end for so many years. Weather the storm. When your prodigal is convinced you are steadfast, he'll finally accept it. He won't like it, but he'll realize you aren't going to back down.

At that point, he has a choice—and his best chance to get out from under the bad habits that have always led to his failure. He can adjust his expectations and establish a new relationship with you based on honesty and respect. And perhaps he can look candidly at his own life, genuinely repent, and turn to God for healing and hope.

TEST YOUR CHILD'S SINCERITY

Many of us are thrilled when we hear a prodigal say, "I'm sorry. I'll never do it again." Parental instinct drives us to let down our guard and trust him, but we need to be a bit more careful. Actions speak much more loudly than words. We can be happy for the good intentions he expresses, but we must also witness genuine change that is worthy of trust. No matter how our prodigals respond, we can offer forgiveness. But trust must be earned over time. Our beloved prodigals need to prove they are trustworthy.

Joseph was sold into slavery by his brothers, taken to Egypt, falsely accused of adultery, and thrown into prison. He languished there for years until God sent the Pharaoh's baker and cupbearer to prison. Joseph interpreted their dreams, and later, when the Pharaoh was troubled by dreams, the cupbearer told him about this remarkable young man. Joseph interpreted Pharaoh's dreams and was rewarded by being made second in command over all of Egypt.

> **But trust must be earned over time. Our beloved prodigals need to prove they are trustworthy.**

Famine hit the land, and eventually Joseph's brothers stood before him (without realizing who he was) to buy grain. In numerous conversations, Joseph tested them repeatedly and specifically to see if they had changed since the days long ago when they had betrayed him. He even threw them in prison for three days, and ordered all but one to return to their father and bring back their youngest brother, Benjamin.

The brothers felt pangs of guilt and speculated that God was chastening them for betraying Joseph. Joseph heard their expressions of grief and guilt, though they had no idea he understood them. Still, he kept testing them. They passed a test of honesty involving a silver cup hidden in their grain. And later at a feast, Joseph arranged for Benjamin to receive five times more food than any of the others to see if the older brothers would reveal any hidden jealousy. This time, they passed the test. They seemed to have changed since the days their envy had caused them to sell Joseph.

> **Follow Joseph's example. Test your prodigal thoroughly. Institute tests to see if he or she is indeed trustworthy. Don't make any premature assumptions. Be wise, and be specific as you plan your tests.**

But as a final test, Joseph made it appear that Benjamin had committed an offense worthy of death, and the brothers immediately begged to take Benjamin's place. Instead of betraying their brother, they were ready to sacrifice their lives for him. Joseph was finally satisfied that his brothers had truly repented and had proven themselves trustworthy. Joseph then revealed his identity, and reconciliation began.

Follow Joseph's example. Test your prodigal thoroughly. Institute tests to see if he or she is indeed trustworthy. Don't make any premature assumptions. Be wise, and be specific as you plan your tests. The sad fact is that not every prodigal will prove himself to be trustworthy. Many parents make the mistake of trusting too much too soon.

Many of us are hesitant to test others. Perhaps it doesn't seem like testing and forgiving can go hand in hand, or maybe we're afraid we will discover that our prodigals really don't want a relationship with us after all. Some of us believe that when we forgive, we must also trust the person. That simply isn't true. We are commanded to forgive because it frees us from being haunted by bitterness and because it puts us in touch with the heart of God. But trust must be earned. We can institute tests, just as Joseph did, to determine the degree that people are worthy of our trust. (As thrilling as it is for you to eventually discover your prodigal to be trustworthy, you can bet your prodigal will be even more thrilled to learn that fact about himself or herself!)

IS IT EVER APPROPRIATE TO GET INVOLVED AGAIN?

Having said all these things, we also need to acknowledge there might be times when it is good and right for you to step in and help your prodigal again. Just be careful that you are acting appropriately. Don't rescue your prodigal if his predicament is the result of sin or irresponsibility. But if he has a car accident or similar problem, for example, helping him is a loving response. (The situation gets a bit more awkward if the accident is the result of his drunk driving. In that case, you may want to offer physical assistance, but not financial help.)

If the prodigal is a son-in-law or daughter-in-law, try to relieve your child's suffering without bailing out the prodigal. In-law issues can be particularly difficult because any direct help you provide for your child is care the prodigal should be providing. The best way to help your child in such cases might be to obtain emotional and relational help from a pastor, counselor, or lawyer to help the child find meaning, purpose, sanity, and direction for the future.

Another time to step in is if your grandchildren are being neglected in any way. If they need food or clothing, take the items directly to their house. (Don't just give money to your son or daughter.) Spend time with your grandchildren, yet try to avoid perpetuating your prodigal's irresponsibility. As much as possible, don't let your grandchildren suffer. Be there for them. Get advice from your friend, counselor, or pastor about your role in a delicate situation like this.

Some parents plead, "Can't I help out my prodigal one more time? This will be the last one. I promise." If you choose to step in "one more time," that's up to you, but don't continue the process of rescuing indefinitely. It is important to communicate your intentions to your prodigal. State your decision clearly, and stick to it.

Significant change can be terribly threatening. Think and pray diligently to get God's perspective. Learn what love really is, even if it must be "tough." Let God produce genuine convictions in your heart that will equip you to get beyond the guilt you are likely to feel when you take a stand. Communicate your decision clearly, and stand strong in the face of opposition. You risk seeing your prodigal walk away, but you also provide the opportunity for genuine repentance and reconciliation. It's worth it.

1. Review the reasons we rescue our prodigals. In what ways can you relate to each of the following?

    — Their failures make us look bad.

    — We hope they'll love us for helping them.

— They demand our help.

— We are motivated by tremendous guilt.

2. What patterns do you detect in your prodigal's prob-
    lems? What patterns do you see in the ways you
    attempt to fix those problems?

3. In what ways have your attempts to fix problems been a hindrance to God's redemptive work in your prodigal's life?

4. Has this chapter given you a fresh new perspective on rescuing your prodigal? If so, how?

5. Write out your analysis and plan:

   How have you been irresponsible in fixing the problems?

How has that hurt your prodigal?

In what ways does your prodigal need to be more responsible?

What are your decisions about what to do (or not do) from now on?

How will your prodigal probably respond to your decision?

How will you respond to his reaction?

6. Who can best support you during this time?

7. What tests can you implement to see if your prodigal is becoming more trustworthy?

⬙

PRINCIPLE #5: GUARD YOUR WORDS

*T*he older lady looked at me like I was a green alien from Mars. She was incredulous. She had begun to tell me about her son's explosive temper and all the pain it had caused, and I had simply asked her, "What do you appreciate about your son, Mark?"

"Appreciate?" She shook her head. "Well, Phil, I'm not sure I can think of a single thing. Mark has messed up his own life, his family, and my life, too. As far as I'm concerned—and I hate to say this about my own son—he's a first class jerk."

I had a sneaking suspicion she didn't hate saying it all that much. She continued telling me her son's story. Mark kept his temper under control most of the time, but only barely. When it blew, it was like a volcanic eruption devastating everything in its path! His wife Beth or their two children could say something they thought was inno-cent, but if Mark was having a bad day, they'd better watch out!

Beth tried to talk to his mother a time or two about the fear she and the kids felt around Mark. His mom told him, "Mark, I'm ashamed of you. You are ruining your marriage, and you're a terrible father. You'd better change your ways right now!" But of course, this "encouragement" didn't make him more compliant. Instead, his rage became even more intense.

To everyone else, Mark seemed to be the picture of Christian maturity. He sang in the choir and prayed fervently in prayer meetings. He went on the men's retreat and sang a solo that almost moved some of those crusty guys to tears.

Yet one day Mark walked in and told Beth he couldn't stand being married any more because her complaining had gotten the best of him. She was stunned. She pleaded with him to stay and promised to change, but his mind was made up. He moved out that day and rented a furnished apartment across town.

Beth went to his apartment that night to try to talk him into coming back home. The door was opened by a friend of Mark's named Martha. Beth was speechless. Martha stammered a weak explanation, but it was clear from the guilt on her face what was going on. Mark came to the door and exploded at Beth, "How dare you come here? You have no business prying into my life!"

"Bu . . . but," Beth stammered as she protested, "but we're still married."

Mark shouted, "Not in my book, we're not!" and he slammed the door.

In a couple of months, the divorce was finalized and the very next day Mark married the "friend." Seven months later, Martha gave birth to an eight-pound baby that was two months premature (if you know what I mean).

During the divorce proceedings, Mark's church had tried to intervene on Beth's behalf. Mark came up with plenty of explanations and accusations, but the pastor refused to overlook the obvious fact that he was committing adultery. Mark left the church, and soon he and Martha joined one nearby. The pastor there was glad to have an accomplished addition to the choir, and he was happy to give Mark and his new bride a fresh start on a new life together. Mark starred in musicals, and Martha sang in the choir, too. While Mark seemed to be doing just fine, Beth and the children struggled.

But Mark wasn't doing just fine. About a year after the birth of their child, Martha went to their pastor and told him horror stories of Mark's explosions at her and the baby. She was terrified of him, and she didn't know what to do. The pastor was shocked, and asked Mark to come in for counseling. Mark arrived the next day with Martha, and he was the picture of repentance and meekness. The pastor felt that God had worked a miracle. But the very next week, Martha called the pastor again in the middle of the night to tell him she had called the police to protect her and the baby from Mark's rage. The judge issued a restraining order to keep him away from them for a month.

It was at this point that Mark's mother was telling me his story. After she finished, I asked her the same question I had asked at the beginning, "I understand that your son has made some terrible mistakes. But what is one quality that you appreciate about him . . . one strength you see?"

> She said, "Phil, you just don't understand. My son is a jerk. Who but a real jerk would treat his wife—actually, both wives—his children, and me this way? There's nothing good to say about him. Nothing at all." Then she had a flash of insight: "If I don't tell him how messed up he is, who will?"

She gave me that same *X-Files* look and began to speak as if she believed I had a single-digit IQ. She said, "Phil, you just don't understand. My son is a jerk. Who but a real jerk would treat his wife—actually, both wives—his children, and me this way? There's nothing good to say about him. Nothing at all." Then she had a flash of insight: "If I don't tell him how messed up he is, who will?"

Some of us become so upset with our prodigals that we are consumed with thoughts about how they are messing up their lives . . . and ours. We can talk for hours about all the details of their faults, but we can't think of much good to say about them.

Our words have great power—either to heal or to destroy. James wrote:

"The tongue is a little member and boasts great things. See how great a forest a little fire kindles! And the tongue is a fire, a world of iniquity. The tongue is so set among our member that it defiles the whole body, and sets on fire the course of nature; and it is set on fire by hell. . . .

But no man can tame the tongue. It is an unruly evil, full of deadly poison. With it we bless our God and Father, and with it we curse men, who have been made in the similitude of God. Out of the same mouth proceed blessing and cursing. My brethren, these things ought not to be so" (James 3:5-6,8-10).

Our thoughts influence our words. If our thoughts are negative, our words will be full of condemnation. If our thoughts are hopeful, we will find affirming words to say. The problem, of course, is that many of us have lost hope. We are so deeply hurt, and our prodigals have been in the far country so long, that we have given up.

In order to think more positively, we need God to refresh our hearts with His great grace. God can and will use anything—absolutely anything—for good if we trust Him. If your prodigal disregards His blessings, perhaps the hard times will get his attention. God is at work whether we can see His plan or not, and He is near whether we can sense His presence or not. Trusting that God is sovereign and good changes our mental outlook. A negative, critical, harsh attitude is eroded away by positive thoughts about God's character and His desire for us and for our prodigals.

> **Our thoughts and hearts reflect bitter hopelessness, so our mouths utter harsh statements. We have said them a thousand times until they feel right.**

MESSAGES WE SEND

Some of us are so angry and hurt that venom just spills out of our lips. We don't try to be critical; it comes naturally. Our thoughts and hearts reflect bitter hopelessness, so our mouths utter harsh statements. We have said them a thousand times until they feel right. They reflect what we truly believe, but they are devastating to us and to our prodigals.

Here are a few statements I've heard parents say to their children:

- "You'll never make anything of your life."
- "I've tried so hard, but now I just can't stand you!"
- "You're not as sweet and loving as your sister."
- "I hate to say it, but I wish you'd never been born."
- "You're such a jerk!"
- "I don't even want to be seen with you."
- "You're such an embarrassment to me."
- "How could you be so stupid?"
- "I don't know what to think about you anymore."

Many of us recognize the destructive power of words like these, so we don't use them. Instead, we are much more subtle. I overheard a man talking to his son and a friend. His son had recently lost his job, and the father was very embarrassed. He had tried to help his son get a new job, but nothing had worked out yet. The friend was talking about his terrific job: a good salary, benefits, three weeks of vacation, and on and on. When the friend finished, the father looked at the ground and said, "Well, son, if you had played your cards right at your old job. . . ."

The son had obviously heard plenty of "ifs" and "buts" from his dad over the past few weeks. He sighed, "I know, Dad. I know I've messed up my life. You don't have to keep reminding me." The father's words weren't terribly harsh, but they were like Chinese water torture: constant dripping that eventually wore his son down.

Quite often, criticizing others is a way of controlling them. If we put them down, maybe they will feel guilty enough or intimidated enough to do what we want them to do. Criticism exalts us as it puts others down. We become masters at identifying anything and everything that is "wrong" with somebody else: their clothes, their hair, where they go on vacations, the way they talk, their hobbies, their church attendance, and even the way they sing "Just As I Am." Misery loves company: If we don't have joy, we resent people who do. We criticize them in an attempt to bring them down to our level of despair.

Let me share some principles about how you can guard your thoughts and speak words of life instead of death, light instead of darkness.

CORRECT SPARINGLY

The main communication principle in almost all relationships is *to correct sparingly and affirm specifically.* We'll first focus on correction.

Don't nag your kids. Don't tell them what they are doing wrong and what you disapprove of. They already know that!

189

Make a list of the messages you have spoken or written to your prodigal during the last month. Which ones have been affirming? Which have been critical of him and his behavior? In addition to any outright condemnations that come to mind, also consider those that are underhanded and subtle.

There is a big difference between correction and criticism. The purpose of criticism is to tear down or control. We use it to hurt a person who has hurt us, or to make her feel guilty so she will do what we think is right. Even as we accuse our prodigals of being manipulative, we try to manipulate them through criticism.

Correction, in contrast, is not self-focused. Its goal is real change, and its motive is hope. We must use correction sparingly and choose our words carefully so they will have power. Occasional correction can open hearts; too much hardens them.

Don't nag your children about their church involvement—or lack of it. I've known some parents who called their adult kids on Sunday afternoon to say, "I noticed you weren't in church this morning." (Their prodigals hadn't been in church for ten years, so I'm not sure what the parents were expecting!) I've known other parents who tried to put the squeeze on their children by telling them, "We're having a special program next Sunday, and I promised the pastor you would be there. Don't let me down." Invite your children back to church, but don't nag them or pressure them. And when they show up, don't make a big deal of it. Just say, "I'm glad to see you. I hope you enjoyed the service."

My father tells a story about a prodigal young man whose mother attended the Brush Arbor Revival Meetings each year. She seldom went to church, but she always "got right with God" during the revivals. As soon as they were over, however, her life always returned to its normal state of apostasy. Her son showed up at the revival one night, and this woman was so excited! At the end of the meeting, she ran down the aisle and told him, "Come on, Son. I want you to go to heaven with me!" He calmly replied, "That's all right, Mom. I won't go tonight because you'll be going back again next year, I'm sure."

Also don't make a habit of correcting or criticizing your child's spouse. If you plant seeds of discontent about your son-in-law or daughter-in-law, you could damage the relationship more than you realize. If your daughter complains to you about her husband, don't reply, "I told you he was no good. If you had listened to me, you'd have dumped that bum a long time ago!" You may feel very negative emotions about your child's spouse, but it's not your responsibility to share them all. At the right time and place, you may have the opportunity to express yourself honestly to attempt to correct a wrong that you see in their relationship. But even then, speak sparingly and wisely.

AFFIRM SPECIFICALLY

A man who had been away from God decided to surprise his mother and go back to church. When his mother walked in that Sunday before the service and saw him sitting in her pew, she looked up and said to everyone there, "Oh, my Lord, you all better run. The ceiling is going to fall in! My son has come to church today!" She wanted to be cute and funny in encouraging her son, but he was deeply humiliated.

We have addressed the necessity of affirming our prodigals. Here, I want to encourage you to do it specifically. Ask God for wisdom about what you might say, and look hard for things your prodigal does well. For instance:

- If he's a good golfer, talk to him about his latest round and tell him he's terrific.
- If she has gotten a promotion at work, tell her how proud you are of her.
- If your son takes his children to the zoo, tell him how much you appreciate his attention and love for his kids.
- If your daughter volunteers at the hospital, tell her you are impressed with her kindness.
- If she prepared dinner, tell her she's a wonderful cook.
- If your son repaired his car, compliment him on his ingenuity.

Focus on the things your prodigal enjoys. And don't just use affirmation as a wedge to get close enough to pounce and say something corrective. Speak affirming words clearly, and avoid any subtle jabs.

DON'T CRITICIZE YOUR CHURCH

Sometimes parents are critical of the very people God uses to bring His grace into the life of the prodigal. I talked to a young man who had gotten far from God and far from his father, who was a music minister. The young man desperately wanted to find some common ground with his dad. He had been spending some time with another man in the church who, unknown to the dad, was gently and lovingly showing him the love of Christ and answering his many questions. I told this young man I would pray that he and his father would be reconciled.

> **And don't just use affirmation as a wedge to get close enough to pounce and say something corrective. Speak affirming words clearly, and avoid any subtle jabs.**

A few weeks later, I was at the church to speak. That night, while the three of us were eating dinner together, the father verbally berated the son's new friend. He said that the man was ungodly and selfish because he hadn't supported a raise for the staff at the last finance committee meeting. I watched the father destroy in five minutes all that God had been doing to bring light into this young man's heart.

You may be angry at your pastor, but don't be calling him names around your prodigal. You may not like the music that was played last Sunday, but don't complain just because it wasn't to your personal tastes. You may be angry at God, but take it up with someone who can help you reason through your anger—not someone who has his own issues with God. The people and functions of your church may be the very tools God is using to bring your prodigal back to Himself. Don't let your critical words—even if they're true—postpone God's work in his life.

SOWING AND REAPING

The law of sowing and reaping operates in every area of our lives, including the words we use and how we use them. When we sow seeds of criticism, nagging, and condemnation, we reap a harvest of bitterness and distance in relationships. But when we sow seeds of love and affirmation, the harvest is one of hope and acceptance.

Are your words seeds of hope or despair in the heart of your prodigal? You are making an impact one way or the other. I encourage you to try two experiments. First, ask ten people for an analysis of how you communicate with your prodigal or about your prodigal. (Most of them will probably tell you only what they think you want to hear unless you assure them that you want their frank, honest answers.) Ask your volunteers to remind you of specific times when you said things to your prodigal which they overheard, or when you spoke about your prodigal to them. Don't defend yourself. Listen to what they say and ask follow-up questions, such as, "How do you think that made her feel when I said that?" or "Did that statement make you think less of my son?"

The second experiment is more significant. Ask your prodigal to tell you what messages you have communicated to him in the past few years, the past few months, and even the past few days. Your prodigal may not want to incur more criticism, so he may be very reluctant to respond. Assure him that you won't argue, and that you'll listen carefully to whatever he says. You may be surprised to find that some of the messages you thought were most hurtful didn't have much impact, and others you thought were minor caused a lot of pain.

Use these two experiments as opportunities for repentance. If you discover that your words have sown seeds of hurt, ask for forgiveness—from God, from your friends, and from your prodigal. From this moment on, determine to speak only words that edify.

Do you remember the encouragement Paul gave to the Ephesian believers? He told them, "Let no corrupt communication proceed out of your mouth, but what is good for necessary edification, that it may impart grace to the hearers" (Eph 4:29). In other words, stop letting your words tear people down, and be sure they build people up instead. No matter what it takes, do it. Repentance is a courageous and continuous act. Trust God for wisdom and power to fulfill His calling to be a healer with your words.

> **The vast majority of what we communicate to others is found in our facial expressions and gestures.**

Words are certainly important, but we also need to remember that studies have shown that 93 percent of communication is nonverbal. The vast majority of what we communicate to others is found in our facial expressions and gestures. If you say, "I love you" with a warm smile and outreached arms, the message rings true. But if you say the same words with a scowl on your face and your arms crossed, the recipient might doubt your sincerity.

Some of us force ourselves to say the right words, but our prodigals see contradictions communicated on our faces and in our body language. They can tell our words are not genuine. In such cases, we have taken a step backward, not forward. We have eroded trust rather than building it.

Think about the nonverbal messages that accompany the words you speak. Do you roll your eyes? Do you turn your back? Do you scowl or wince? Your body language is very important. Become a student of it. Learn, change, and grow.

BE PATIENT

Jesus used agrarian metaphors not only because most people were farmers, but also because they communicate realities of life very effectively. A farmer doesn't plant today and expect a harvest tomorrow. The growing cycle requires lots of time, so the wise farmer is both careful and patient. He plows and prepares the ground in the spring. He plants the seed and then prays for good weather as they begin to sprout. If he gets sufficient rain and sun, and if storms don't devastate the crop, he can harvest in summer or fall.

Not only do we reap what we sow, but we find other parallels between sowing seeds of grain and sowing seeds of love and hope in the lives of our prodigals. For example, we shouldn't expect a prodigal to change simply because we speak one kind word after years of criticism. Just as hard earth must be plowed before it is conducive for the growth of seeds, a hard heart must be softened before it is receptive to seeds of hope. It is far more realistic to expect to speak many positive words over a long period before we expect any results.

We need to "plow" our own hearts to prepare them and allow God to work through us with compassion rather than criticism. Then, as we sow seeds of love in the hearts of our prodigals, we need to wait patiently for those seeds to take root. Many of our children have become skeptical of kind words, and rightly so. They wonder if we will go back to our old habits of nagging and condemning.

Many of our prodigals will wait to see if we really mean what we say. If we are consistent in expressing love, they may respond with joy and thankfulness. They won't necessarily repent of their sins on the spot, but they will be less resistant to change. The prostitutes and tax collectors who gathered around Jesus didn't comprehend His message right away, but they felt His love and wanted to be near Him. As they spent time with Him, His grace and truth rubbed off on them.

> **Many of our prodigals will wait to see if we really mean what we say.**

Some studies indicate that it takes 14 affirming statements to overcome a single negative one. Many parents reverse this ratio. If we want our prodigals to listen, we must use correction only when it is accompanied by grace and love, expressed both verbally and nonverbally.

BE ACCOUNTABLE

Changing years of bad habits is not easy. We need wisdom, courage, and others who care enough to hold us accountable. Your spouse, a good friend, or your pastor may be able to fulfill that crucial role for you. Ask the person to give you a signal (a hand motion or a simple word) to let you know when you are off base again in conversations with your prodigal. Invite that person to speak honestly to help you uncover motives and emotions that drive your actions. Deal with your hurt and disappointments, your anger and humiliation. As God works deep in your heart, your perspective will gradually change and your messages to your prodigal will change, too. But during this time of reflection, determine to speak words of kindness no matter how you feel. It is right. It is good. It pleases God.

> "What if I don't *feel* like saying affirming things to my prodigal? If I say them anyway, isn't that hypocrisy? Phil, you know how Jesus felt about hypocrites."

KINDNESS IS A CHOICE

Some parents challenge me: "What if I don't *feel* like saying affirming things to my prodigal? If I say them anyway, isn't that hypocrisy? Phil, you know how Jesus felt about hypocrites. I sure don't want to be one of them!"

It is certainly laudable to live in integrity and avoid hypocrisy, but God calls us to obey Him even when we don't feel like it. Jesus pleaded with the Father to let Him escape the horror of the cross, and His prayer was so intense that sweat fell from his brow like drops of blood. He knew the intense pain He would experience, yet He submitted to the Father's will. I believe it is the Father's will that parents speak words of grace to their prodigals, even when they don't feel like it. The commands in Scripture are clear. We are to forgive, be tenderhearted, and speak only those words that build up.

Kindness is a choice, not a feeling. If you still feel angry, take your anger to God and let Him give you insight and healing for the hurt you feel. Don't let your anger be an excuse for withdrawing, condemning, or nagging your prodigal. Choose to do what God commands, no matter what.

A dear lady was deeply disappointed in her son, and she had often communicated her disappointment in words, facial expressions, and body language. But she accepted my challenge to speak words of grace to him. She was still angry at him for foolish decisions he continually made and gambling away his money, but she determined to start affirming him. She prayed and asked God to show her something—anything—he did well. A few things came to mind: his diligence at work, his beautiful rosebushes, and the way he helped her when her old car needed repairs. She also realized she needed to stop nagging him about not coming to church, his frequent trips to the dog track, his choice of friends, and the way he treated his ex-wife and kids. She determined to bite her tongue about those things and focus on the good.

She started with, "Son, I appreciate all your hard work at the office. I'm sure you're doing a good job there." To be honest, her words sounded as contrived to her as they sounded foreign to her son. In the past she had complained that he spent so much time at work that he neglected his kids. He didn't know how to take this unexpected compliment, so he mumbled, "Thanks," as he waited for the other shoe to drop. It didn't.

A few days later, she commented, "I hope your roses will be as pretty this year as they were last year." Again, he expected this to be only a ploy to start a conversation so she could drop verbal bombs about his gambling, but she changed the subject to her own garden.

Months went by as she stuck to using only positive comments. She told me, "I'm not sure if the change affected him, but it sure affected me! When I stopped dwelling on his faults, I felt freer and more relaxed. And believe it or not, I actually enjoyed seeing him again."

After several more months, the plowing, sowing, watering, and waiting finally bore fruit in her son's life. One day he told her, "Mom, I don't know what happened, but you've definitely changed. At first I thought you were putting me on. I didn't believe you appreciated anything about me. But I guess you do."

His mother's eyes filled with tears as he continued. "Mom, why don't you come over and help me cut some roses? I think they'd look good on your dining room table."

Her son didn't stop gambling that day, and he didn't come back to church that next Sunday, but he and his mother began a new chapter in their relationship, one based on respect, kindness, and love. And what do you know? About a year later, someone sat down beside her in church during the first hymn. She turned and saw her son smiling at her. He had chosen to be in church with her instead of going to the track. "Glory to God!" she thought.

> **But he and his mother began a new chapter in their relationship, one based on respect, kindness, and love.**

A C L O S E R L O O K . . .

1. In your personal experience, how would you confirm James's statement that "the tongue is a fire" (James 3:6)?

2. What are some recent verbal messages you have given your prodigal? Can you think of any nonverbal ones? How did he or she respond to each one?

3.   What are some specific things you appreciate or admire about your prodigal? (Think of work, talents, hobbies, relationships, and any other area of life.)

4.   Talk to ten people and ask them what messages you have communicated to or about your prodigal. Summarize their comments below.

5.   Ask your prodigal what messages you have communicated to him or her. Write a paragraph here to summarize what you learn from the conversation.

6. What specific steps will you take to stop speaking destructive words and start (or accelerate) the use of affirming words?

7. In terms of a farmer's expectations and patience, what can you expect as you try to relate more positively to your prodigal?

PRINCIPLE #6: PRAY SPECIFICALLY

"$\mathcal{P}$hil, I've prayed for my son every day for his entire life, for 53 years now. I enjoyed praying for him while he was in school. When he joined the Navy and got involved in drinking, I prayed even harder. During the last 25 years, I've prayed over and over again for God to change his heart, but nothing has happened. I still pray, Phil, but now they're just words. I've stopped expecting an answer."

Many parents can identify with this mother. She is a devout Christian who loves God with all her heart, but she can't understand why God hasn't answered her prayers. She praised God for His deliverance on the occasions when her son told her he had stopped drinking, but he always started again. She thanked the Father for His mercy when her son came back to church, sat next to her, and sang the hymns like he did when he was a boy. But he didn't keep going long.

"I'm about prayed out, Phil," she almost whispered.

People have always struggled to hang on to their faith. Mark records a confrontation between Jesus and the father of a demon-possessed boy:

"And they brought [the boy] to Him. And when he saw Him, immediately the spirit convulsed him, and he fell on the ground and wallowed, foaming at the mouth. And He asked his father, 'How long has this been happening to him?' And he said, 'From childhood. And often he has thrown him both into the fire and into the water to destroy him. But if You can do anything, have compassion on us and help us.' Jesus said to him, 'If you can believe, all things are possible to him who believes.' And immediately the father of the child cried out and said with tears, 'Lord, I believe; help my unbelief!' When Jesus saw that the people came running together, He rebuked the unclean spirit, saying to him, 'You deaf and dumb spirit, I command you, come out of him, and enter him no more!' And the spirit cried out, convulsed him greatly, and came out of him. And he became as one dead, so that many said, 'He is dead.' But Jesus took him by the hand and lifted him up, and he arose" (Mark 9:20-27).

> **I want to encourage you to be honest about your struggles with unbelief, just like the father was honest with Jesus, but don't give up.**

Parents of prodigals sometimes feel the frustration of the father in this story. They have tried everything they know to do, and they have prayed for years. They believe in God, but their faith has wavered. They no longer believe that God is going to work in their prodigals' hearts.

I want to encourage you to be honest about your struggles with unbelief, just like the father was honest with Jesus, but don't give up. Keep trusting our merciful and sovereign Lord to accomplish His purposes. Let me offer some prayers to help you pray more specifically.

"LORD, USE MY PRODIGAL'S FRIENDS"

In my conversations with prodigals who had returned to the Lord, I asked, "Who had the greatest influence to convince you to turn back to Christ?" To my surprise, it wasn't the parents. The primary positive influence on prodigals is their friends who care enough to speak the truth and take them to church. Prodigals expect their parents to push and pull them toward God, so they often disregard them as an influence. But a coworker, a friend, a neighbor, or someone who is a member of the same club can often find a prodigal's listening ear that has been closed to parents.

My encouragement, then, is for parents to pray, "Lord, would You bring a godly friend into my prodigal's life to share the message of hope and model a life of trust in You? Bring somebody who will love my prodigal with Your love and melt his heart with Your grace."

When your prodigal tells you that he went to church down the road with a friend, don't give him a lecture about how he should have come to your church. A friend of mine prayed daily and diligently for 20 years that his son would get right with God. In answer to his prayers,

God worked in the son's life. A man he worked with shared the gospel with him, and he became a Christian. The son started attending an Assembly of God church with his coworker, and he really grew in his faith.

But my friend, the boy's father, attends a Baptist church. He took his son aside and scolded him, "Son, I'm ashamed of you! How could you go to an Assembly of God church when you know I disapprove of the way they do things?"

I'm sure the Son of God rejoiced that the man's son had come to faith, but the father had a different agenda. Being a Baptist, it appeared, was more important to him than being saved.

When this son told me this story, I could tell he was heartbroken by his father's harsh words. I gave him a hug and told him, "My friend, your dad is wrong about this. I'm so proud of you for walking with God. And I'm thrilled that God has led you to a church where you are being encouraged in your faith. Maybe someday your dad will understand this, too."

Some parents try to put the squeeze on their kids if they attend a different church while they are still searching for God. Sometimes I hear, "Phil, we need my son at our church. I don't know why he'd go to that other one."

Don't get your priorities (and God's priorities) mixed up. God is much more concerned with the condition of your child's heart than with which pew supports the seat of his pants. If God uses another Bible-believing church down the street to influence your child for the Kingdom, be glad for him or her. It may be a different church, but it's the same Kingdom.

Please don't interfere with the work of God in your child's life. Rejoice that your prodigal is interested enough to go to church anywhere at all! Thank God for your prodigal's friend, no matter what evangelical church he attends.

And if you have the opportunity, make a point of thanking the friend for being an answer to prayer. Thank him for letting God use him to be such a positive influence on your child. Don't make a big deal of it.

> ...Make a point of thanking the friend for being an answer to prayer. Thank him for letting God use him to be such a positive influence on your child.

You may not even want your prodigal to know you are thanking the other person. But let the friend know you'll keep praying for both him and your prodigal as they walk with God together.

"LORD, CHANGE ME FIRST"

In these pages, we have already mentioned the need for us to look inside our own hearts to address the resentment and disappointment that is a part of being the parent of a prodigal. It is much easier to focus on all the changes our prodigals need to make. But we need to begin by praying, "Lord, work in my heart. Even if my son or daughter never changes, change me."

I am encouraged as I read the psalms. David and the other psalmists expressed their hearts openly to God. They didn't sugarcoat how they felt or what they believed. They were painfully honest and direct in addressing God. Many of the psalms express deep disappointment and heartache. David wrote,

"How long, O Lord? Will You forget me forever?
How long will You hide Your face from me?"
(Ps 13:1)

As the psalmists were honest with God, He met them at their deepest point of need. He reminded them of His goodness and sovereignty. We don't know how long the process of encouragement took, but the psalms almost always end with expressions of hope and trust. After David poured out his anguish to God, he found refreshment in God's wisdom and love. See how he finished the psalm:

"But I have trusted in Your mercy;
My heart shall rejoice in Your salvation.
I will sing to the Lord,
Because He has dealt bountifully with me"
(Ps 13:5-6).

Most of us have prayed for years that God would change our prodigals. Perhaps we need to pray that God will change us first. Perhaps God wants to work on our bitterness, and give us the grace to forgive. Maybe God wants to ease our pain by having us confront our grief and disappointment. Maybe God wants to deflate our sense of self-righteousness and remind us that He is God, not us. Maybe God wants to replace our hopelessness with joy and thankfulness.

Our prodigals surely need the touch of God, but perhaps we need to feel it first. Then, as God works His kindness and healing in our hearts, our faces and our words can better reflect God's love to our prodigals and to everyone else around us.

> **Most of us have prayed for years that God would change our prodigals. Perhaps we need to pray that God will change us first.**

"LORD, GIVE ME A FRESH PERSPECTIVE"

We often quote Romans 8:28, but do we really believe that "all things work together for good to those who love God, to those who are the called according to His purpose"? We wish God would just answer our prayers and fix things. We wish our prodigals would repent and our families would be united in peace and love. That's how we would work things together for good, isn't it?

But God's ways are full of irony. I'm convinced that His purpose is not necessarily to make our lives happy, but to do whatever it takes to convince us to trust Him. Our pains and failures are tools in His hands as they turn our thoughts toward Him. C. S. Lewis called pain "God's megaphone" to get our attention, so instead of trying to avoid pain at all costs, and whining when we don't get what we have prayed for, we can ask God for a fresh perspective.

The pains we experience highlight our need for God. The longing we have for a child to return to God (and us) is the very thing that makes us depend on Him. When we are weak, our faith can become strong. We are embarrassed by the foolish things our prodigals have done, but that foolishness is an opportunity for God's wisdom and power to shine. In the midst of all the darkness, God may even choose to use you and me to bring His light to someone we love.

Physician and psychologist Paul Tournier wrote about this irony:

> "The most wonderful thing in this world is not the good that we accomplish, but the fact that good can come out of the evil that we do. I have been struck, for example, by the numbers of people who have been brought back to God under the influence of a person to whom they had some imperfect attachment. . . . Our vocation is, I believe, to build good out of evil. For if we try to build good out of good, we are in danger of running out of raw material."[4]

Rather than becoming obsessed with the evil around you, ask God to give you a fresh perspective to see how He can bring good out of it. Look for the hand of God in your difficult situations. He is willing to use even the most horrible sins and the most foolish choices, as long as we trust Him to do just that.

---

4 Paul Tournier, *The Person Reborn* (New York: Harper & Row, 1966), pp. 80-81.

"LORD, I ASK FOR BROKENNESS"

It is a dictum of Alcoholics Anonymous that a person has to "hit rock bottom" in order to change. We are prideful people. We don't want to admit our needs, and we try to compensate for our shortcomings however we can. Your prodigal is no different. She will cling to any hope of fooling herself, her friends, and her family as long as she can. Most prodigals don't look for help until they become very needy. In fact, as I watch people in trouble, I am convinced that the only factor that determines whether someone gets help is utter desperation. When people become genuinely desperate, they will cling to anything that promises the hope of change. Before they reach that point, however, they use all kinds of excuses and mind games to convince themselves that they're doing just fine.

A friend of mine has a sister who is an alcoholic. He has tried to talk to her about Christ over and over again since high school when he became a Christian, but she would never listen. She made fun of him to her friends, but nothing could stop him from loving her. They are now in their 40's, and he still prays for her every day. He asks God to touch her heart, break through the hard shell of her pride, and draw her to Himself. He prays for her brokenness.

Over the years, she has had four failed marriages, two miscarriages, a bout with cancer, and a near-fatal car accident. In each case, people told her, "Wow! You are so unlucky! Look at all the bad things that have happened to you." But my friend believes God has been answering his prayers. Each calamity has brought an opportunity for her to "come to her senses" and repent. Each heartache has been God's megaphone to get her attention. But so far, she has kept her hands over her ears.

"I don't know what it's going to take for God to get through to her," he told me sadly. "But there's one thing I'm sure of: God is sure doing His job of giving her chances to repent. I couldn't ask Him to be any clearer in showing her the desperate needs in her life. Maybe some day she'll listen."

> **Before you and I feel sorry for the hard times our prodigals go through, maybe we should ask, "God, is this Your way of getting his attention?"**

Before you and I feel sorry for the hard times our prodigals go through, maybe we should ask, "God, is this Your way of getting his attention?" If it is (and I believe every difficulty is exactly that), then we'd better not fix their problems. Instead, we'd better let God have His way in our prodigals' lives.

"LORD, HELP ME FIGHT THE BATTLE"

Make no mistake: You and I are in a spiritual battle all day every day. The forces of evil are strong, but they are nothing compared to the incredible power of God. Our dear prodigals may be in the grip of evil, but God is far stronger.

Christians tend to make one of two mistakes when we think about the devil. We either don't think about him enough, or we think he has more power than he actually does. We know he is a thief who "comes to steal, to kill, and to destroy." He delights in deceiving our prodigals about the goodness of God, and he delights in deceiving us about God's gracious intentions. If he can make us question God's character, he gains a foothold he can exploit.

We resist him with truth and grace, with the Word of God and with the power of love. Paul reminds us:

"[God] raised [Jesus] from the dead and seated Him at His right hand in the heavenly places, far above all principality and power and might and dominion, and every name that is named, not only in this age but also in that which is to come. And He has put all things under His feet, and gave Him to be head over all things to the church, which is His body, the fullness of Him who fills all in all" (Eph 1:20-23).

Jesus isn't "barely" above the forces of darkness; He is "far" above them. He is infinitely more powerful, and He has given us tremendous resources for the battle we fight. Later in the same letter, Paul instructs us to fight and to use all the armor available to us (Eph 6:10-20). Soldiers in battle expect to get dirty and even to be wounded from time to time, but if their resources are good and their commander is a great leader, they are con- fident of victory.

When you pray long and hard, yet despair that your prayers haven't been answered, you're in good company. The prophet Daniel once prayed for three weeks for

God's help. Finally, the angel Michael appeared and explained that God had heard his prayer the first time he uttered it, but an adversary had blocked the path of the help God had sent.

> **Ask God to give you a fresh perspective on spiritual conflict so you can fight more faithfully and effectively for your prodigal.**

God hears every prayer, but Satan remains active in attempting to block God's good work. Your prayers are essential for your victory and the successful return of your prodigal, even though it may seem you have been praying in vain. Ask God to give you a fresh perspective on spiritual conflict so you can fight more faithfully and effectively for your prodigal.

"LORD, DON'T LET ME GIVE UP"

Some of us have wrestled with our hurt and guilt in connection to our prodigals for so long that we are tempted to just give up. We've had it. We've tried being nice. We've tried being tough. We've listened to the advice of friends. We've prayed a million times for our prodigals to change. But nothing has worked.

The fruit of the Spirit includes the quality of "long-suffering." Tenacity is one of the primary virtues in the Christian life. We are urged to "run with endurance the race that is set before us" (Heb 12:1).

I have never run a marathon, but those who have tell me that at various times in the race, they want to quit. Their legs feel like lead, their stomachs ache, vision gets blurry, and they are nauseated. The feel like they can't take another step, but they take that one . . . and the next. (And it's something they do for fun!)

The Christian life is similar. It's a marathon, not a sprint. Jesus is our supreme example of tenacity. We are encouraged to keep "looking unto Jesus, the author and finisher of our faith, who for the joy that was set before Him endured the cross, despising the shame" (Heb 12:2). Jesus could endure the worst that life had to offer because He knew what would come later: resurrection and reunion with the Father. As we follow His example, we need tenacity and guts to keep going, to keep believing that God is good and that He is sovereign. Even when we see no visible evidence, we can trust His word that He is at work.

"LORD, WHATEVER IT TAKES . . ."

While our eyes are on Jesus and His supreme example of sacrifice, we begin to see the value of brokenness. Parents need to be willing to pray, "Lord, I will do whatever it takes for my prodigal to respond to You." In Paul's letter to the Romans, he expressed a passionate hope for his kinsmen's salvation:

> "I tell the truth in Christ, I am not lying, my conscience also bearing me witness in the Holy Spirit, that I have great heaviness and continual sorrow in my heart. For I could wish that I myself were accursed from Christ for my brethren, my kinsmen according to the flesh" (Rom 9:1-3).

217

Doesn't this sound like the desperate plea of a parent of a prodigal? Paul speculated about going to hell if that act could achieve salvation for the people he loved. No sacrifice was too great, including the exchange of his own salvation for theirs. Can you say the same about your commitment to your prodigal?

I grew up in a solid, secure family as an only child, and yes, I was spoiled rotten. We had none of those "dysfunctional family" problems you hear so much about these days. My parents were very loving, and I was a happy kid. As a boy, our family attended my mother's home church. She was one of 11 children, and with the exception of one brother, all of her living siblings still attend that same church.

My mother's oldest brother is Charlie, nicknamed Bud. Uncle Bud was old by the time I grew up, but I loved to spend time with him. He was a godly man who loved to pray. When I went into the ministry, I had an office behind my house and Uncle Bud often stopped in to see me. Sometimes he'd say, "Phil, I need us to pray about something. Will you pray with me?" I was always delighted to pray with him.

One time he told me through tears that one of his grandchildren had a brain tumor. I knew Uncle Bud was serious about prayer when he wanted to kneel. He was crippled in one of his legs, so it was quite an ordeal for him to get on his knees, but that was the desired position for the kind of praying Uncle Bud wanted to do. We prayed for his grandson that day, and God miraculously spared his life. Uncle Bud came a couple of other times when there was conflict in the church. He didn't want my advice; he just wanted me to pray with him.

One day Uncle Bud came by for a casual visit, but as we talked the conversation turned more serious. He told me he had four children who were all walking with the Lord, but a few of his grandchildren had turned their backs on God. It broke his heart. He loved those young people, and he wept as he talked about their lives. They were doing some things that would embarrass other parents or grandparents and evoke sharp criticism, but Uncle Bud never criticized them. He just loved them. We knelt and prayed that day for his dear grandchildren.

> **Uncle Bud never criticized them. He just loved them. We knelt and prayed that day for his dear grandchildren.**

One of them was named Marla. When she was in college, Marla walked away from the Lord. After her graduation, my Uncle Bud (Marla's grandfather) got very sick with cancer. During his illness, he kept loving Marla and showing great kindness to her. His love melted her heart, and she came back to God.

One day Marla gave her testimony in a weekly chapel service and told about how that special man had loved her when she didn't even love herself. He had prayed for her when others criticized her. He had smiled when others had frowned. As he lay dying of cancer, she remembered that he didn't talk about himself. When she went to see him, he only wanted to talk about her life and what she was interested in. God touched her heart through her old, sick grandfather.

Marla blessed the name of God with her story. I sat there thinking how proud her grandfather would have been if he could have heard her. That afternoon when I left the office, I glanced over to where my old office had stood when Uncle Bud was alive and he used to come see me. I remembered his prayers for her. At that moment I prayed, "Lord, if You see my Uncle Bud walking around heaven today, would you tell him that his Marla blessed Your name today? I think he'd enjoy hearing about that. Tell him his prayers have been answered."

If you have read this far into this book, you obviously have a deep commitment to love your prodigal, and you probably are praying for your dear son or daughter like Charlie prayed for Marla. I wish I could give you a guarantee that your prodigal will respond, and I wish I could give you a formula that is sure to work, but I can't. What we can do is say to God, "Lord, I want to be an instrument to do all I can to bring my child back to you. I'm willing to live, and I'm willing to die. I'm willing to be rich or to be poor. I'm willing to live in pain if that's what it takes for you to work deeply in my life and pour out Your love on my child. I'm Yours, Lord. Do whatever it takes."

Someday after you are gone, you just may be walking around heaven and hear the Lord say, "I've got great news to tell you. Your prodigal has come home!" What a wonderful day that will be!

A CLOSER LOOK . . .

1. Describe the history of your prayers for your prodigal. When have you felt confident of God's hand at work? When has your faith wavered?

2. Write your own prayer according to these openings:

    — Lord, use my prodigal's friends.

    — Lord, change me first.

— Lord, give me a fresh perspective.

— Lord, I ask for brokenness.

— Lord, help me fight the battle.

— Lord, don't let me give up.

— Lord, whatever it takes . . .

CHAPTER 9

Two Joys

*N*ancy stood with her daughter Christy as she told me about her relationship with her 45-year-old son, Rob. "I loved him so much that I closed my eyes to all he was doing wrong. When I finally saw things clearly, I hated him. He was a mess. So was I. As a boy, he was the 'golden child,' cute and funny. Everybody said he had the most wonderful personality, and they were right. I guess we bragged on him too often." Nancy's voice trailed off for a moment, then she continued. "It really went to his head. By the time he graduated from high school, he thought he was the center of the universe. I guess he was, in our family at least."

Christy added, "I sure loved my older brother. Rob was so handsome. He looked just like Elvis, even in high school. The girls thought he was the cutest! We had a lot of fun together. We teased each other all the time, and for a little sister, that was something special. And Rob was really protective. I never had to worry about guys treating me badly. A time or two, Rob followed through with his threats to protect me. I'll tell you, that sure made an impression on me—and on everybody else at the school. I loved him so much."

Nancy then told me the reason she had wanted to talk to me. "After Rob graduated from high school, he was so self-centered that everybody and everything had to revolve around him. He got married, but when his wife didn't worship him . . . well, the way Christy and I did, he divorced her. He married somebody else and soon divorced her for the same reason. Over a period of 15 years, he got married six times, but three of those marriages were to the same woman. I guess she kept thinking things would change. They didn't."

Nancy stared at the ceiling a few seconds before continuing. "When he was a boy, we never wanted him to be unhappy. We gave him whatever he wanted, so Rob never developed an ability to handle money. By his second or third marriage, he was also in trouble financially. He started a business, which—I heard from a reliable source—he burned down so he could collect the insurance. The police suspected him, but he got away with it. He started gambling to try to make a lot of money fast. He won sometimes, and felt that he was on top of the world, but far more often he lost everything he had at the blackjack table."

Another pause, and Nancy continued, "Did I mention that he beat his wives? It's remarkable that the same woman went back to him for the third time. It looks like I raised a monster, doesn't it? But I couldn't see it. I told myself for years and years that all his problems were somebody else's fault. I tried my best to help him. I gave him advice about the women he was going with, but he married them anyway. I would ask him to come over and fix something at my house when I knew he was planning to go to the casino, but he caught on and stopped coming.

"He only came to church when he was scared to death about something, like when one of his wives asked for a restraining order or when he thought he'd had a heart attack. At one point, he had two sons born during the same week—one from a previous wife and the other with his current wife. So he didn't want to talk to me about anything having to do with God."

Nancy now spoke in somber tones, "As I look back, he was domineering even as a boy. I overlooked it because he was so smart and good-looking. But when something didn't go his way, he pouted or threw a tantrum or something. Christy was the first to see the problems developing, but when she tried to talk to me, I wouldn't hear a word of it. I thought she was betraying Rob by saying bad things about him. I hate to say it, but it literally took me *years* to wipe away the scales and see the truth. Rob is a selfish, hardhearted, violent bum. And when I finally saw the truth, I hated him. For many years I was enraged at him, but I also felt ashamed. I couldn't believe that he was so selfish, and I couldn't believe I had helped produce that monster."

Christy gave her mother a hug as Nancy told how she had found some peace. "I stopped talking to

I hate to say it, but it literally took me *years* to wipe away the scales and see the truth. Rob is a selfish, hardhearted, violent bum. And when I finally saw the truth, I hated him.

Rob for a long time. I refused to go to one of his weddings, and I sure didn't want to get involved in any of his problems any more. I was furious. Christy had been trying to help Rob, but she realized long before I did that trying to control him wasn't helping him or us. When she stopped, I first thought she was being selfish, but as time went on, I saw she was right. Blindness had been my problem for years, followed by a long period of bitterness. I desperately needed some peace. Christy helped me learn to forgive Rob, to stop fixing his problems, and to love him without expecting anything in return. It's been hard, but God has forgiven me for treating Rob like an idol, and Christy has forgiven me for preferring him over her when she was little. All I can do now is to live each day trusting God to give me wisdom and joy, and that's exactly what I'm doing. Rob hasn't changed, but I have. I now have joy in my life that I never had before, and it's wonderful!"

Nancy and Christy embraced like two war veterans at a reunion. They had been in the trenches, facing bullets of anger, hurt, and manipulation. And they had come through the fight together.

Parents of prodigals can seek two joys. One is God's response to their faithfulness, and the other is the possible return of their prodigals. Let's look at those joys.

OUR FAITHFULNESS

Nancy understood and experienced the first of these two joys. When we are following Christ and doing what He wants us to do, He is pleased. The day will come when you and I stand before Christ and He will ask us about our lives as believers. This event is described in Paul's first letter to the Corinthians, and it is commonly called "the judgment seat of Christ." Our deeds as believers will pass through the flame of judgment. Those done for selfish reasons will burn, but those done for Christ's glory will endure and be rewarded. Paul wrote,

> "Each one's work will become manifest; for the Day will declare it, because it will be revealed by fire; and the fire will test each one's work, of what sort it is. If anyone's work which he has built on it endures, he will receive a reward. If anyone's work is burned, he will suffer loss; but he himself will be saved, yet so as through fire" (I Cor 3:13-15).

On that day, God will look at our hearts and our faithfulness. He won't be asking you and me about our prodigals. He'll be seeing our perseverance to trust Him even when our prodigals didn't come home. If we are faithful, we will hear those wonderful words, "Well done, good and faithful servant. Enter into the joy of your Master." I long to hear those words, don't you?

Our obedience is what will be evaluated. Did we trust God and speak truth? Did we stop withdraw-

> **If we are faithful, we will hear those wonderful words, "Well done, good and faithful servant. Enter into the joy of your Master." I long to hear those words, don't you?**

ing and move toward our prodigals in strong love? Did we look for what we can affirm instead of what we so easily condemn? Did we make the hard choice to thank God even when things looked bleak? Did we keep praying even when we saw no answers? Did we help other parents of prodigals who were struggling to find hope and meaning? None of us does these things perfectly, yet as we practice we get a lot more consistent.

To remain faithful, parents of prodigals need the deep and strong hope that God will accomplish His purposes, even if His purposes aren't exactly like ours and are on His timetable rather than ours. Our hope cannot depend on the responses of our prodigals. It must be founded on the character of God Himself.

Psalm 130 contains a beautiful description of this kind of hope. The psalmist compares his trust in God to a lookout on the wall of a besieged city. The greatest danger occurs during the night when the enemy can sneak up close to the walls. The lookout peers intently into the darkness, watching and longing to see that first ray of light in the east that means day is coming and he will be able to see far more clearly. The psalmist writes:

"I wait for the Lord, my soul waits,
And in His word I do hope.
My soul waits for the Lord
More than those who watch for the morning—
Yes, more than those who watch for the morning"
(Ps 130:5-6).

In the Scriptures, the idea of "waiting" implies a strong hope, an expectation that something will happen. We "wait for the bus" not simply because we would kind of like to have a bus come along, but rather because we've seen it come before on a regular schedule and believe we can count on it. And we "wait on God" because we have learned to trust the consistency of His faithfulness and character. Sometimes we wish God had a schedule we could figure out, but in fact, God's schedule is often maddeningly slow from our perspective. Yet we can be certain that He will eventually come.

In the meantime, our souls wait in eager expectation for the God of the Universe, the One who is both good and sovereign, to shine His light on our hearts. Like a lookout on the city walls, we may be under attack and in the darkness, but we can trust that God will soon enough provide the light we need. It takes great faith to wait for the Lord. Even our expectation that He will bring light sooner or later is an evidence of our trust in His goodness and grace.

> **It takes great faith to wait for the Lord. Even our expectation that He will bring light sooner or later is an evidence of our trust in His goodness and grace.**

Another encouraging passage is Jeremiah's statement of confidence in Lamentations. Jeremiah was surrounded by prodigals! The entire nation of Israel was a prodigal country, but the prophet riveted his eyes on God's grace, and he found peace there. He prayed:

"Remember my affliction and roaming,
The wormwood and the gall.
My soul still remembers
And sinks within me.
This I recall to mind,
Therefore I have hope.
Through the Lord's mercies we are not consumed,
Because His compassions fail not.
They are new every morning;
Great is Your faithfulness.
'The Lord is my portion,' says my soul,
'Therefore I hope in Him!'
The Lord is good to those who wait for Him,
To the soul who seeks Him.
It is good that one should hope and wait quietly
For the salvation of the Lord"
(Lam 3:19-26).

Jeremiah didn't sugarcoat his predicament. He experienced affliction, bitterness, and gall. He was deeply discouraged. But he didn't wallow in hopelessness. Instead, he used his predicament as a starting point to remember the goodness of God. He realized he could be consumed by his heartache, but he chose to focus on God's love and faithfulness which was "new every morning." He waited expectantly, hoping that the God who is far above all would meet him in the quietness of his heart.

Jeremiah is a model for us to remain faithful in hope. His experience was dark and foreboding, but he trusted God. In the same way, being the parent of a prodigal is often a bleak venture, but we too can trust God. We don't know if our prodigals will repent, and we don't know if they will ever change—but we can. We can remain faithful even when those around us are faithless.

Your prodigal will have to account for his own choices before God's throne. His or her mistakes won't be held against you. Instead, the Lord will look at you and ask, "Did you trust Me? Did you love the unlovable and forgive the deep hurts you experienced? Did you reach out? Did you treat your prodigal like an adult instead of like a child, expecting him to act responsibly?"

God doesn't expect perfection. He only desires honesty, a contrite heart, and genuine efforts to make progress in relationships. If we take steps to obey Him, we will hear those wonderful words, "Well done, good and faithful servant." God will be pleased, and we will bask in His smile.

THEIR REPENTANCE

Some prodigals never return. Some come back for good. Some return for a while, to the joy of their parents, but are drawn back to the "far country" and leave their parents weeping again.

We can't force a prodigal to repent. The best we can do is act like the father in Jesus' story and long for the prodigal's return. If we see him coming down that long road toward home, we can run to embrace him and let the celebration begin!

God is willing to use every situation, no matter how tragic, to bring reconciliation between prodigals and their

> God is willing to use every situation, no matter how tragic, to bring reconciliation between prodigals and their parents.

parents. Rachel had gotten pregnant in high school, and her father was so ashamed of her that she moved out of the house. She simply couldn't stand his scowls, sighs, and constant "I told you so's." She had her baby and named him Johnny, but her father refused to see either one of them. When the rift between Rachel and her father failed to heal, she moved to a city several hours away. Through the next 12 years, her mother maintained contact, but her father remained totally estranged. Time only deepened his bitterness and shame.

One day her mother called Rachel to say that her dad had been in a terrible car accident. He was in the hospital, near death. She wanted to go to his bedside, but assumed she would be the last person on earth he would want to see. To her surprise, her mother told her, "Rachel, your father wants to see you . . . and Johnny. Can you come?"

She grabbed her almost-teenager, jumped in her car, and sped across the state to the hospital. As they approached her father's room in ICU, she swallowed hard and knocked on the door. Her mother's voice said, "Come in." Rachel went in and saw her father with tubes in his chest and wires hooked up all over his body. Her mother smiled and motioned for them to come to his bedside. Her father smiled as he reached out and touched her hand. Tears streamed down his face, then hers and her mother's. Her father tried to speak, but Rachel told him, "Not now, Daddy. You can tell me later."

He shook his head, "No," he whispered, "this has taken way too long already. Rachel, I'm so sorry. Will you please forgive me for being so unkind to you and Johnny?"

Rachel wept as she nodded her acceptance of his apology. Through her sobs, she told him, "Daddy, I was wrong, too. Will you forgive me for getting pregnant?"

The sobs of joy were so loud that a nurse burst into the room to see what was wrong. "Nothing's wrong," Rachel's mother told her. "We're a family again." The nurse smiled as she backed out of the room.

God uses all kinds of things to bring families back together. Sometimes He uses the broken hearts of the prodigals, and sometimes He uses the broken hearts of the parents. Sometimes He uses tragedies to mend hearts and homes. I'm convinced that God is very much at work to give us opportunities to respond to Him. Rachel's father's heart was hardened until he faced death. At that moment, God melted his resistance and he reached out to his daughter and grandson. Reconciliation had begun.

Throughout this book are stories of prodigals. As I think back on scores of conversations with men and women who turned their backs on God, I can see the faces of many who have come home. But I'm also reminded of the faces of those who, for whatever reason, chose to stay in the hog pen, hungry and alone.

When the Prodigal Son returned, his father ordered the servants to put the best robe on his shoulders, a ring on his hand, and sandals on his feet. He killed the fattened calf and prepared a great feast, "for this my son was dead and is alive again; he was lost and is found."

It bears repeating that each of these items symbolized the father's acceptance of his son. The robe was reserved for important guests. It signified dignity. The son may have still smelled like the hogs he had been feeding, but the father immediately bestowed dignity on the one who had none.

The ring was a symbol of authority, of sonship restored. This young man had squandered every possession and every cent of his inheritance. In coming home, he only desired to be made a hired servant under his father's roof, but his father returned him to a place of prominence as his dear son.

The sandals signify status. Only slaves and servants went barefooted, as the young man probably was when his father embraced him. The boy expected to remain unshod as a hired servant, but the father ordered that the sandals of status be given to him.

The fattened calf was reserved for the most important celebrations. The father saw his son's return as the greatest blessing he could experience, one he had prayed for during all the months and years his son had been away. Now it was time to celebrate, and no expense would be spared. Joy overflowed from the father's heart during this most special occasion of all.

If your prodigal returns, don't spare the joy—experience it in its fullness. Don't remind him of the stupid things he did while he was away, and don't beat yourself up for not being the parent you should have been. Live in the joyous present, not in the shameful past. Follow the father's example, and give wonderful gifts of love to show your acceptance to your returning prodigal.

Your prodigal's repentance is the beginning of a journey of reconciliation. There will be (not *might* be) adjustments to be made on both sides. The relationship can't go back to "the way it was before," but it can become far better than it ever was before. You will have more insight into yourself, your prodigal, and God's faithfulness, and your returning prodigal should appreciate your love more now than ever.

> **Your prodigal's repentance is the beginning of a journey of reconciliation. There will be (not might be) adjustments to be made on both sides.**

As you show your care consistently, any doubts your prodigal has about the sincerity of your love will disappear. The first days and weeks may be awkward, as they were when the Prodigal Son's elder brother began to speak his mind. Expect some tensions and misunderstandings during those first encounters. Address them calmly and deliberately, just as the father in Jesus' story addressed the anger of his older son.

Things will never be the same. They will be better. Let God continue to work His goodness and grace deep into each person's life until His wisdom and joy permeates your family. And give thanks that your prodigal has come home.

I think often of the ten lepers who came to Jesus for healing. He told them to go to the priest, and on the way they were healed of their disease. All ten were made well, but only one came back to thank Jesus for what He had done. "Where are the others?" Jesus asked. Thank God often for doing what no one else could ever do, for bringing light out of darkness in your prodigal's heart.

I HOPE FOR YOU . . .

Paul and Silas were on an exciting adventure responding to Christ's command to take the gospel to the entire world. In Europe they found a woman, Lydia, who trusted Christ as her Savior. As Paul continued sharing the gospel with people, things were going as they had envisioned.

Then some men came along with a demon-possessed slave girl. The demon in this girl spoke out and distracted the people who were listening, so Paul cast the demon out of her. Her owners had been making money from the fortune-telling she did through her demonic powers. They weren't happy with Paul and Silas, so they dragged them to the authorities. Here's what happened next:

> "Then the multitude rose up together against them; and the magistrates tore off their clothes and commanded them to be beaten with rods. And when they had laid many stripes on them, they threw them into prison, commanding the jailer to keep them securely. Having received such a charge, he put them into the inner prison and fastened their feet in the stocks" (Acts 16:22-24).

This was not at all what Paul had planned! He and Silas were trying to do exactly what God led them to do, and now they found themselves beaten bloody in the innermost dungeon of the city prison with their feet fastened in stocks. They could have looked at their situation and complained, "God, how could You allow something like this? Being in prison can't be what You want. Get us out of here right now!" And they could have blamed each other. Silas could looked over at Paul and griped, "If you hadn't cast that demon out of the slave girl, we'd be telling people about Jesus right now instead of being stuck in the bottom of this hole, bleeding on everything!"

Paul and Silas, however, made a different choice:

"But at midnight Paul and Silas were praying and singing hymns to God, and the prisoners were listening to them. Suddenly there was a great earthquake, so that the foundations of the prison were shaken; and immediately all the doors were opened and everyone's chains were loosed" (Acts 16:25-26).

Instead of blaming God, Paul and Silas trusted that His ways were far higher than they could imagine. When the situation was darkest (it was midnight in the deepest dungeon), they held onto the hope that God is good and sovereign. Though they didn't understand God's plan, they trusted that He had one, and that it was a good one. They sang hymns, prayed, and praised, even though they

> **When the situation was darkest (it was midnight in the deepest dungeon), they held onto the hope that God is good and sovereign. Though they didn't understand God's plan, they trusted that He had one, and that it was a good one.**

had no idea how their situation would turn out. In their case, God performed a miracle. An earthquake freed all the prisoners, and many more people came to Christ after seeing the power of God.

Parents of prodigals are, in many ways, in the same situation that Paul and Silas were in. They only wanted the best and never planned for their kids to become prodigals. They didn't ask for the pain and darkness that descended on their hearts and their families. They feel trapped, stuck in a spiritual and emotional hole. Yet they, too, have a choice. They can fixate on what they wanted for themselves and their children as they gripe and whine. Or they can cling to the goodness and sovereignty of God, trusting that He understands. Even as they are confused in the darkness, they can pray, sing hymns, and praise God for His faithfulness.

That is your choice and mine—every day. I believe God will work a miracle of hope and healing in your heart, and perhaps, in the life of your prodigal.

I hope God has used this book to encourage you. If you haven't worked through the questions at the end of the chapters, I hope you will go back and do so. Stop focusing on what your son or daughter needs to do. Start with personal self-examination and see what you can do instead. Stop trying to change or blame other people. Assigning blame may make you feel better for a little while, but it won't solve the problem.

Allow the Holy Spirit to shine His light on your heart and show you what—if anything—you have done wrong in this relationship. The devil uses guilt to keep us depressed, and depression makes us ineffective in the Lord's work. Ask God to give you insight and honesty. As you experience God's forgiveness, you will become willing and able to forgive your prodigal and ask for his forgiveness.

Pray for courage, but don't try to figure everything out on your own. We are "the body of Christ," and we need each other, especially when we are struggling. You may need to find a Christian counselor and read additional books to learn how to respond to your prodigal's situation. Your child may need professional help—a doctor, a counselor, or a lawyer—to handle his problems. In any case, he will need your moral support. As you interact with him, ask the Lord for an encouraging heart instead of a condemning heart.

Find friends who have prodigals, and start a support group to pray for each other's sons and daughters. Their understanding and encourage-

> **That is your choice and mine—every day. I believe God will work a miracle of hope and healing in your heart, and perhaps, in the life of your prodigal.**

241

ment is tremendously important during this time. No matter how long he has been gone, cling to the hope that one day your prodigal will come home. If you ever lose that hope, you'll give up. And always be willing to say, "Lord, whatever it takes, I'm willing to do it."

Some day you may look down that dusty road and see a familiar figure in the distance, and you'll rejoice that your prodigal has come home.

A CLOSER LOOK . . .

1. Have there been times in your relationship with your prodigal when you have been tempted to give up on God and stop trusting Him? Describe some of those times.

2. How does the idea of "waiting on the Lord" encourage you to hang on and keep trusting Him? (Review Psalm 130.)

3. How does it change your perspective to know that someday you will stand before Christ and give an account of your own trust, attitudes, and actions rather than your prodigal's?

4. Think about Paul and Silas in the deepest part of prison, beaten and bloody, with their feet in stocks. How does their situation compare with yours as a prodigal's parent? How does praising instead of complaining affect your outlook?

5. As we conclude this book, write a prayer to God expressing:

    — Your thankfulness for His goodness.

    — Your desire to trust Him no matter what.

    — Your reluctance to apply any of the principles in this book. (Be specific.)

— Your desire to please God by your faithfulness.

— Your hopes for your prodigal.

USING *PARENTING PRODIGALS* IN CLASSES AND GROUPS

This book is designed for individual study, classes, and small groups. The most powerful way to benefit from these principles is for each person to study and apply the reflection questions individually, then to discuss them in a group setting.

Your church may want to conduct a class on Sunday mornings or on a weekday evening. A pastor or another skilled communicator can teach these principles over 8 to 12 weeks. Of course, the nature of our relationships with our prodigals is complex and difficult, so it may take more than once through the material for some people to grasp and apply it. That's entirely understandable and appropriate. I suggest that your church conduct these classes back to back over the course of the year. In most cases, those who go through once will want to go through it again because their first exposure will raise new questions.

The questions and exercises at the end of each chapter aid reflection, application, and discussion. Order enough copies of the book for each person to have one. For couples, I strongly encourage both husband and wife to have a book so both can record their thoughts and prayers.

A recommended schedule for a class might be:

Week 1	Introduction to the material where the teacher can tell his own story, share his hopes for the group, and provide books for each person
Week 2	Chapter 1
Week 3	Chapter 2
Week 4	Chapter 3
Week 5	Chapter 4
Week 6	Chapter 5
Week 7	Chapter 6
Week 8	Chapter 7
Week 9	Chapter 8
Week 10	Chapter 9
Week 11	Questions and Answers: specific questions that people want to talk about
Week 12	Stories of Hope: participants share stories of how God has worked in their lives, and in their prodigals' lives

Let us share your burden

Being the parent of a prodigal is not an easy burden to bear, but our hearts are encouraged when we know someone is bearing the burden with us through daily prayer.

Phil Waldrep and the staff of Phil Waldrep Ministries considers it a high honor and a holy privilege when parents, grandparents, siblings or friends ask us to pray for their prodigals. So, this is our commitment to you:

If you write us and share your request with us, we will pray with you for your prodigal. When you write, you may tell us as little or as much as you would like for us to know. We promise to add your prodigal to our prayer list for thirty days. And, don't forget to share your story with us when the prodigal comes home. We want to rejoice with you!

Send your prayer request to:

Phil Waldrep
Phil Waldrep Ministries
P.O. Box 148
Trinity, Alabama 35673-0148

Phil Waldrep is a man with a heart for people. His passion to share the gospel and provide resources for believers to grow in their relationship with God began when he was a young man.

Phil gave his life to Jesus Christ when he was seven years old. Nurtured by the faith of the rural Baptist church he and his parents attended, Phil began seeking God for his guidance in choosing a career. He then realized the Lord was calling him to full-time ministry.

By age eighteen, Phil was speaking regularly in churches across the south. He formed the Phil Waldrep Evangelistic Association in 1980 to broaden his ministry and fulfill his vision.

© Charles Seifried

252

*T*oday, Phil receives numerous requests to speak. His yearly schedule includes invitations to many of the leading churches across North America.

A leading expert on senior adult issues, he enjoys interacting with and communicating to that audience. Each year, Phil speaks to dozens of senior adult conventions, leads churches in senior adult revivals, and addresses many of the leading organizations and corporations in the world. His unique blend of humor, insight and communication skills make him a repeat guest.

Phil married the former Debbie Gray in 1984. They have two daughters, Maegan and Melodi, and make their home in Decatur, Alabama. He is a graduate of the University of Alabama and the Luther Rice Theological Seminary.

If you would like to know more about Phil Waldrep Ministries or how you can have Phil speak to your church or organization, contact:

> Phil Waldrep
> Phil Waldrep Ministries
> P.O. Box 148
> Trinity, Alabama 35673-0148
> (256) 355-1554

© Charles Seifried

*P*hil Waldrep Ministries is a non-profit

organization committed to sharing the gospel by every means, traditional and non-traditional, and to provide quality resources for believers to grow in their relationships with God, their families and their friends. In addition to books and tapes, the ministry conducts major conferences, including:

Senior Adult Celebrations!

Senior Adult Celebrations! are events designed for retirees and senior adults. Held in major tourist areas, the

© Charles Seifried

Celebrations feature many of America's leading preachers, musicians, comedians and Christian celebrities. Among those who have appeared are Dr. David Jeremiah, Mark Lowry, George Beverly Shea, and Art Linkletter.

Women's Weekend Getaways

Women enjoy getting away with friends and focusing on their relationships with each other and the Lord. That is why the Women's Weekend Getaways are popular events for Christian women. The retreats begin on Friday night and conclude Sunday morning. They feature some of the most popular women speakers in the country.

Mountain Top Men's Retreat

Men from across the country gather each Spring for the Mountain Top Men's Retreat in Talladega, Alabama. The weekend event motivates men to develop their relationship with Christ, deepen their love for their family, and work more effectively in the local church.

Oasis Summer Student Camps & Student Celebrations!

Phil Waldrep Ministries joins hands with church youth ministers to provide a fun-filled, spiritually enriching week for high school and college students each summer. Oasis camps feature special guests, exciting worship, Bible studies and messages designed for today's teen. In addition, the camps feature special activities that cause teens to grow closer to God, their friends, family and church. The Student Celebrations! are designed to encourage and motivate students in their walk with God.

If you would like to know more about any of our exciting conferences, contact our office for a free brochure.

Phil Waldrep Ministries ▪ (256) 355-1554

Books make great gifts!
Order for yourself or a friend

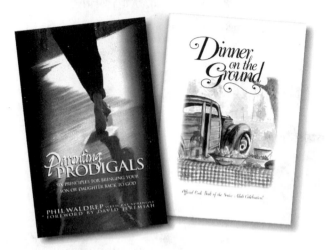

"Dinner on the Ground" Cookbook
Special recipes from attendees at the Senior Adult Celebrations!
$19.95

"Parenting Prodigals"
Six Principles for Bringing Your Son or Daughter Back to God
$19.95

Also available:
Parenting Prodigals
45-minute Cassette Message by Phil Waldrep
$5.00

Postage & Handling (first book)......................... $4.00

Postage & Handling (each additional book)........ $2.00

Postage & Handling for cassette .... Free

If you wish to order by credit card call: (256) 355-1554
Make checks payable to Phil Waldrep Ministries
We accept: Master Card, Visa, American Express, Discover